HUGH CARPENTER & TERI SANDISON

Hot Vegetables

TEN SPEED PRESS

Berkeley, California

Ten Speed Press
Post Office Box 7123
Berkeley, California 94707

Distributed in Australia by Simon & Schuster Australia, in Canada by Ten Speed Press Canada,
in New Zealand by Tandem Press, in South Africa by Real Books, in the United Kingdom
and Europe by Airlift Books, and in Singapore and Malaysia by Berkeley Books.

Cover and book design by Beverly Wilson.
Typography by Laurie Harty.
Typefaces used in this book are Avant Garde, Futura, and Opti Vanilla.

Library of Congress Cataloging-in-Publication Data
Carpenter, Hugh.
Hot Vegetables/Hugh Carpenter & Teri Sandison.
     p.   cm.
Includes index.
ISBN 0-89815-975-X
1. Cookery (Vegetables) 2. Cookery, International. 3. Spices
I. Sandison, Teri II. Title.
TX801.C337   1998
641.6'5--dc21

                                      98-17031
                                      CIP

First printing, 1998
Printed in Hong Kong

1 2 3 4 5 6 7 8 9 — 02 01 00 99 98

All blessings to our mother earth

Contents

Hot Vegetables Night After Night ... 8

Grilling, Roasting, and Broiling ... 10

Stir-Frying ... 12

Sautéing ... 14

Steaming, Poaching, and Blanching ... 15

Tempura and Deep-Frying ... 16

Microwaving and Pressure-Cooking ... 18

Vegetable Stocks ... 19

Artichoke TO Zucchini

Beans: Fresh Fava Beans, Lima Beans,
  and Soybeans   26
Chiles   40
Greens and Leafy Salads   54
Hot New Asian Vegetables   58
Mushrooms   64
Root Vegetables   84
Winter and Summer Squash   92

Glossary   106
Artists' Credits   108
Acknowledgments   108
Conversion Charts   109
Index   110

Hot Vegetables Night After Night

Come with us and share the harvest of the garden. Never before in America has there been such a profusion of fresh vegetables. Across the country, in the produce sections of markets, it is common to find giant portobello mushrooms, asparagus flown in from Chile, baby lettuce greens year-round from local farmers or from growers in California, and an array of Chinese vegetables that a decade ago would have been found only in Chinatown markets in a few large cities.

Witness the burgeoning trend in farmers' markets. Speak with avid cooks from any community—no matter how small—and they will tell you of the locations and times of nearby farmers' markets, which roadside stands should never be passed without a visit, and new ways to cook the common, the heirloom, and the new.

Hot Vegetables is for everyone who loves vegetables, whether strict vegetarians or those who want exciting vegetable side dishes. It's a book for noncooks to use to learn simple ways of preparing the wide variety of readily available vegetables, and it's a book for creative cooks who want to add new impact to vegetable creations.

Organized alphabetically, from **Artichoke** to **Zucchini**, the recipes in **Hot Vegetables** use some of our favorite flavor ideas and cooking techniques from around the world to give new twists to foods from the vegetable kingdom. Dip artichoke leaves into a spicy mayonnaise sauce of grated orange, ginger, cilantro, and chiles. Simmer mushrooms with oyster sauce, thyme, and garlic, then toss with pasta. Boil fresh English peas in their pods, and then purée and strain the peas to create a brilliantly green, fresh pea soup. Brown yellow onions before simmering them in a sauce of cream, vermouth, and fresh tarragon, and later cover the stew with a buttermilk biscuit crust and bake until golden. Smoke thickly sliced tomatoes on the outdoor grill, then chop and simmer with coconut milk, basil, and chile to make a sauce that transforms pasta from the ordinary to the divine.

Join us to celebrate the bounty of the garden. Create new twists with old vegetable favorites. Surprise your family and friends with simply prepared yet bold and complex-tasting creations. Challenge fixed dietary habits. Educate and tempt your palate. Here is a kingdom worth celebrating every day.

Hugh Carpenter and Teri Sandison

Grilling, Roasting, and Broiling

Grilled, roasted, and broiled vegetables taste sensational. The hot, dry heat from the grill or oven strengthens the vegetables' unique flavors, concentrates the natural sugars, adds a deep low-note taste, and gives vegetables a bold, rustic, and highly appealing look. Serve grilled, roasted, and broiled vegetables hot or chilled as appetizers; add them to salads and soups; take the vegetables straight from the grill or oven and roll them in heated tortillas with added spoonfuls of a freshly made salsa; or use grilled, roasted, or broiled vegetables as a flavorful accompaniment to meat and seafood entrées.

- While all long-cooking vegetables can be cooked entirely on the grill or in the oven, giving these vegetables a preliminary blanching in boiling water greatly shortens last-minute cooking. The blanching can be completed hours in advance. If choosing to cook several types of long-cooking vegetables, such as broccoli, carrots, and cauliflower, blanch each vegetable separately. To blanch vegetables, trim or cut them into sizes suitable for going directly from the grill or oven to the dinner plate. Submerge the vegetables in a generous amount of rapidly boiling water. The moment the vegetables brighten in color, transfer them to a bowl filled with cold water and ice. Once the vegetables are thoroughly chilled, pat them dry and refrigerate them. Use this technique for beets, broccoli, carrots, cauliflower, green beans, potatoes, and yams.

- Marinating most vegetables is unnecessary. Most raw vegetables have a dense texture and will only begin to absorb the flavor of a marinade during cooking. The exceptions are mushrooms and eggplant. Marinate these for at least 5 minutes, but not longer than 30 minutes. Longer marinating causes their texture to turn from pleasant to soggy.

- How long should the vegetables be grilled, roasted, or broiled? Cook the vegetables until they brighten in color, are well heated through, have lost their raw taste, and have become lightly golden. Because vegetables cook quickly, turn them frequently, and brush them often with extra marinade.

- If you plan to serve grilled vegetables with grilled meat or seafood, always grill the vegetables first, then push them to the cooler edges of the grill while you grill quick-cooking fish fillets, shrimp, scallops, and thin steaks. For longer-cooking seafood (whole salmon fillets) and meats (thick steaks, chicken cut into pieces or left whole), remove the grilled vegetables and keep warm in a 200° oven, and then grill the seafood or meat. If serving roasted vegetables with roasted meats, add the vegetables around the sides of the meat during cooking.

Marinade Suggestions: The salad dressings from the following recipes are excellent as marinades brushed across vegetables just before the vegetables are grilled, roasted, or broiled: asparagus and pine nut salad (page 23), beet salad (page 29), endive salad (page 50), fennel root salad (page 52), jicama salad (page 60), radicchio salad (page 82), and tomato salad (page 98).

Vegetables to Grill, Roast, and Broil

Asparagus: Snap off and discard the tough stems. Grill or broil asparagus 3 to 6 minutes on each side, depending on the size of the stalks.

Beets: Grill whole, skin on or off, until tender in the center, about 45 minutes, or cut the beets into ½-inch slices and grill the slices about 10 minutes on each side. If grilling baby beets, place the whole baby beets on skewers and cook them about 8 minutes on each side, or roast the beets in a 400° oven until tender.

Broccoli: Discard tough ends, peel stems, and cut between the florets to separate them. Grill about 6 minutes on each side, or roast in a 400° oven until tender.

Carrots: Peel the carrots. Cut large carrots in half lengthwise. Grill them about 8 minutes on each side. Skewer baby carrots, and grill them about 4 minutes on each side, or roast them in a 400° oven until tender.

Cauliflower: Break cauliflower into large pieces. Grill about 10 minutes on each side until tender, or roast in a 400° oven until tender.

Corn: Cook corn with the husk on or off, about 5 minutes on the grill.

Eggplant: Cut globe eggplant into ½-inch-thick slices; cut Japanese or Chinese eggplant lengthwise into three strips. Marinate 5 to 30 minutes. Grill or broil about 4 minutes on each side.

Green Beans: Discard tough stem ends. Skewer the beans and grill about 6 minutes on each side, or spread them on a baking sheet and roast in a 400° oven for about 12 minutes.

Mushrooms: Choose firm mushrooms (button, cremini, portobello, shiitake, porcini, chanterelles, morels) but not soft mushrooms (oyster or enoki mushrooms). Discard tough ends. Marinate mushrooms 5 to 10 minutes. Grill or broil the mushrooms until they soften slightly.

Onions: Trim the ends off green onions, then grill or broil the onions about 1 minute on each side. Peel yellow or red onions, cut them into ½-inch slices, and grill or broil the slices about 6 minutes on each side.

Potatoes, Sweet Potatoes, Yams: Grill large potatoes, skin on or off, either whole or cut into ½-inch-thick slices. Grill until tender in the center, about 45 minutes for whole potatoes and 10 minutes for sliced potatoes and yams, or cook them in a 400° oven until tender.

Squash, Summer: Cut the squash lengthwise into three strips. Grill or broil the strips about 2 minutes on each side.

Squash, Winter: Peel the squash and cut it into ½-inch-thick slices. Grill the slices about 10 minutes on each side, or roast in a 400° oven until tender.

Sweet Bell Peppers: Stem and seed the peppers and remove the ribs. Grill or broil the peppers about 4 minutes on each side.

Tomatoes: Cut large tomatoes into ½- to 1-inch-thick slices and grill or broil the slices about 2 minutes on each side. Skewer cherry tomatoes and cook them about 1 minute on each side.

Stir-Frying

Woks and vegetables, in the few minutes of their culinary dance, achieve a perfect gastronomic marriage. The searing heat seals the moisture (and thus the vitamins and minerals) within the vegetables, heightens their natural sweetness by caramelizing the sugars, fully cooks vegetables in seconds while retaining their distinctive natural textures, adds a subtle undercurrent of satisfying low flavor notes, and transforms the colors into brilliant hues. Whether served as an important accompanying player to the main entrée or as the centerpiece of a vegetarian meal, stir-fry vegetables always play a starring role.

Key Wok Techniques with Vegetables

The vegetables listed in this section are only suggestions. Choose the freshest vegetables, cut no more than 4 to 5 cups of vegetables into equal-size pieces, then follow the stir-fry rules listed below.

Short-Cooking Vegetables: Add one or any combination of the following vegetables to the hot wok: thin asparagus, baby green beans, Chinese long beans, cabbages (white cabbage, red cabbage, napa cabbage, bok choy), celery, Japanese eggplant cut into $1/4$-inch slices, mushrooms (button, cremini, shiitake, portobello, chanterelle, honey, or morels but not oyster or enoki mushrooms, which become mushy when stir-fried), onions (yellow, red, and white onions, green onions, and chives), peas (garden peas, snow peas, sugar snap peas), peppers and chiles (all the colored sweet peppers, as well as the entire range of spicier peppers and chiles), summer squash (zucchini, crookneck, pattypan and all other squashes that become tender with brief cooking), and fresh water chestnuts.

Long-Cooking Vegetables: Thick asparagus, broccoli, Brussels sprouts, carrots, cauliflower, potatoes, string beans, and yams require longer cooking because of their dense texture. To accelerate the cooking process, cut the vegetables into small pieces suitable for stir-frying, and then briefly microwave them, or blanch the vegetables in boiling water just until they brighten, and then chill the vegetables in ice water. They can now be combined with short-cooking vegetables, not to exceed a total of 4 to 5 cups of vegetables.

Leafy Greens and Bean Sprouts: This group includes all kinds of lettuce, as well as spinach and bean sprouts. Add up to 2 cups of these to any type of stir-fry dish at the very end of the stir-fry process.

How to Improvise Stir-Fry Vegetable Dishes

No cooking technique other than stir-frying allows such a startling range of variations, additions, substitutions, omissions, and outright culinary creativity. Once a cook understands the simple rules, stir-frying becomes an improvisational cooking technique that is ideally suited for today's fast-paced, "eat on the run" society.

Vegetable Stir-Fry Seasonings and Sauces

Wok Seasonings: Stir-fries can be seasoned with any combination of the following: 1 to 2 tablespoons finely minced ginger; 3 cloves finely minced garlic; 1 teaspoon grated orange, tangerine, lime, or lemon skin; 1 serrano chile minced, including the seeds; 1 tablespoon rinsed and chopped Chinese salted black beans.

Coconut Wok Sauce: Combine ½ cup coconut milk, ¼ cup vegetable broth, 1 tablespoon oyster sauce, 2 tablespoons chopped basil leaves or cilantro sprigs, 1 tablespoon dark sesame oil, 2 teaspoons cornstarch, 1 teaspoon Asian chile sauce.

Orange Wok Sauce: Combine ⅓ cup freshly squeezed orange juice, 2 tablespoons dry sherry, 2 tablespoons oyster sauce, 2 teaspoons dark sesame oil, 2 teaspoons cornstarch, ½ teaspoon sugar, ½ teaspoon Asian chile sauce.

Oyster Wok Sauce: Combine ¼ cup vegetable broth, 2 tablespoons oyster sauce, 1 tablespoon dark sesame oil, 2 teaspoons cornstarch, 1 teaspoon sugar, ¼ teaspoon freshly ground black pepper.

The Classic Stir-Fry Order

Cut the vegetables into small sizes suitable for stir-frying, not to exceed a total of 4 to 5 cups vegetables. Prepare a wok seasoning and a wok sauce listed above or from another wok recipe. Here's the wok action:

1 Heat the wok over highest heat until very hot. Add 1 tablespoon of flavorless cooking oil to the center of the wok, and roll the oil around the sides.

2 Immediately add the vegetables and wok seasonings.

3 Stir-fry the vegetables until their color brightens, about 2 minutes.

4 Immediately add the wok sauce. Continue stir-frying until the sauce glazes all the ingredients and thickens slightly, about 1 minute.

5 Transfer the vegetables to a heated platter or dinner plates and serve at once.

Sautéing

Sautéing is a wonderfully easy technique for everyday cooking. It's the perfect technique for making use of extra vegetables and for improvising simple, quick, and delicious vegetable entrées and side dishes. The difference between stir-frying and sautéing is that, for stir-frying, all cooking is done over highest heat, but for sautéing, even if the cooking begins over high heat, the temperature is eventually reduced to medium or low. Cooking chopped yellow onions over low heat until caramelized is sautéing, just as cooking sliced Japanese eggplant briefly over high heat, then adding a sauce, covering the pan, and simmering over medium-low heat until the eggplant becomes tender is another example of this technique.

How to Improvise Sautéed Vegetable Dishes

1. Wash and dry the vegetables. Cut them into any size, provided they fit neatly in the pan.

2. Place a sauté pan over medium-high heat. When it's hot, add 2 to 3 tablespoons of olive oil, a flavorless oil, butter, or a combination of oil and butter.

3. Add minced aromatics such as 3 cloves minced garlic, 1 shallot, 1 teaspoon minced ginger, or any combination of these. Cook for a few seconds.

4. When the aromatics release their aroma into the air, but before they turn brown, add any long-cooking vegetables. Vegetables to consider are listed on page 12. Cook the vegetables until they begin to sizzle in the pan.

5. Add about 1 cup of liquid, such as any one of the following: coconut milk, cream, salsa, tomato sauce, white wine, vegetable or chicken broth. Season the dish with 1 or 2 tablespoons of chopped fresh herbs, or Chinese seasonings, particularly 1 tablespoon oyster sauce and 1 tablespoon dark sesame oil. Cover the pan, turn the heat to low, and steam-cook the vegetables until they become tender. Adjust the seasonings to taste. Serve at once.

6. For short-cooking vegetables, review the list on page 12. Short-cooking vegetables can be added to long-cooking vegetables after the long-cooking vegetables are nearly tender (step 4). Or you can eliminate the long-cooking vegetables. Just add the short-cooking vegetables to the pan after cooking the seasonings (step 3). Cook the vegetables until they sizzle, and then add 1 cup of liquid (step 5). Short-cooking vegetables cook so quickly that it's unnecessary to cover them.

7. Leafy greens and bean sprouts can be sautéed on their own, or 1 to 2 cups can be stirred into the long-cooking or short-cooking vegetables during the last few seconds of cooking. Cook the leafy greens just until they wilt or the bean sprouts become hot.

Steaming, Poaching, and Blanching

Steaming means to cook vegetables on a perforated tray that is elevated above rapidly boiling water in a covered utensil. Because steam is trapped in the pan, its temperature is hotter than that of the boiling water. Thus steamed vegetables cook quicker than boiled or poached vegetables, and they have an enhanced flavor. We use a metal or bamboo Chinese steamer that affords more space to place the vegetables than the little stainless-steel, collapsible steamers designed to fit into saucepans. Steaming vegetables and topping them with melted butter, salt and pepper, a homemade hollandaise sauce, or salsa is a simple, nutritious way to cook vegetables, especially when you want to accent their natural flavor.

Vegetables for steaming can be left whole or cut into small pieces. Choose vegetables that take the same amount of time to cook, which are listed on page 12 under the categories "Long-Cooking Vegetables" and "Short-Cooking Vegetables." Use one or more vegetable combinations within one of those categories. Cut the vegetables into the same size. Place them on a steamer tray, allowing enough room for the steam to circulate through the vegetables. If a Chinese steamer is used, the vegetables steaming on the second tier will be cooked at the same time as those in the bottom tier. The water should be at a furious boil when you add the vegetables to the steamer tier and cover the pot. Maintain the heat on high throughout the steaming process. The vegetables are perfectly cooked when they become brightly colored and are tender. *Caution: Be very careful when removing the steamer lid that you don't scald your hands or face.*

Poaching means to submerge food in water and cook until tender. We've never cared for this technique because the flavor quickly leaches from the vegetables. There is almost always a better method. Avoid this technique, which is perilously close to the dreaded "boiled vegetables."

Blanching means to submerge vegetables into a large quantity of boiling water and then cool them instantly by plunging the vegetables in a large container of iced cold water. This technique is used as a preliminary technique for speeding the stir-fry process. It's also an excellent technique for cooking vegetables you intend to serve chilled as an appetizer or to include in a salad. Consider all the vegetables listed under the category "Long-Cooking Vegetables," page 12. To blanch, trim and cut the vegetables into the desired size. Bring enough water to a rapid boil so there will be plenty of space for the vegetables to "swim." Stir in the vegetables. Since the cooking process is very quick, stir the vegetables continuously. For example, medium asparagus will be done in approximately 30 seconds and broccoli florets take about 1 minute. The moment the vegetables turn a bright color and are tender, tip the vegetables into a colander, and then plunge the vegetables immediately into a bowl of cold water and ice. When the vegetables are chilled, pat them dry, and refrigerate until ready to use.

Tempura and Deep-Frying

Nowhere else in the world has deep-frying been raised to such a gastronomic art as in Japan. The deep-fry technique was introduced to Japan in the sixteenth century by Portuguese traders who popularized batter-fried foods, particularly on religious days known by the Latin name **Quattuor Tempora**. With a little advance preparation, using vegetables at the peak of freshness, and with a willingness to perform brief last-minute culinary work, you can provide your family and friends a sublime taste treat.

Vegetables to consider: whole asparagus with the tough ends snapped off, broccoli florets, carrot strips, green beans, whole green onions, small whole button mushrooms, strips of bell peppers, snow peas with their stems discarded, yams that are peeled and cut crosswise or into strips, and zucchini strips.

Since batter-frying involves last-minute cooking, be prepared ahead of time. Have ready a wire rack resting on a baking sheet lined with paper towels, to place the fried vegetables on. Use spring-loaded tongs or long chopsticks to dip the vegetables in the batter and then into the oil. Make sure the vegetables are completely dry.

Use a heavy 12- or 14-inch frying pan but not an electric frying pan, which does not have the power to maintain the oil at the desired temperature during cooking. Keep the pan handles pointed inward, across the other burners, so there is no chance of accidentally knocking the pan off the stove. If possible, do the cooking outside by placing the frying pan on a portable burner or directly on a gas grill with the heat turned to medium-high.

Restaurants submerge the food in oil—true deep-frying. However, home stoves do not generate the necessary heat to maintain a large amount of oil within the required temperature range of 350 to 375°. If the oil ever cools below this temperature, the vegetables will taste greasy. Therefore, cook only a small amount, or cook in batches. You will need 2 cups of oil for a 12-inch omelet pan, and 3 cups of oil for a 14-inch pan.

Use a flavorless cooking oil that has a high smoking temperature and a thin viscosity, such as safflower oil or peanut oil, but don't use corn oil, which is too "thick," and never use any flavored oils, such as olive, walnut, or sesame oil.

Although the oil will be too shallow for a deep-fat thermometer to provide an accurate reading, there are a number of techniques for judging if the oil has reached the critical 350 to 375° range. A thin slice of ginger or a drop of batter, when dropped into the oil, will rise quickly to the surface and bubble around the edges when the oil is hot enough. But the easiest technique is to place the end of a wood spoon or bamboo chopstick into the oil. If dozens of tiny bubbles immediately rise from around the immersed tip, the oil is at least 350°. *Warning: If the oil begins to smoke, it's far too hot. Immediately turn off the heat and cool the oil.*

Once the oil is at the correct temperature, dip the vegetables one piece at a time into the batter and then into the oil. The moment the batter turns golden, transfer the vegetables to the wire rack.

Serve the food at once. There's no way to keep the batter-fried vegetables warm for even a few minutes. For this reason we prefer to serve them as appetizers. Thus the cook is not drawn away from the dining room table and only needs to cook a small amount.

Sauces to Accompany Batter-Fried Vegetables

Sauces to use include Asian-Cajun Dipping Sauce (page 22) and Spicy Asian Butter Sauce (page 22), the salad dressings from asparagus salad (page 23) and the fennel root salad (page 52), and the salsas on page 99. Or serve with this mixture: ¼ cup thin or low-sodium soy sauce, 1 teaspoon grated orange zest, 2 tablespoons freshly squeezed orange juice, 2 tablespoons unseasoned Japanese rice vinegar, 1 tablespoon light brown sugar, 1 tablespoon finely minced ginger, ½ teaspoon Asian chile sauce, and 1 tablespoon minced green onion, basil, or cilantro. For "heat," stir in 1 teaspoon Japanese horseradish (wasabi) until smooth.

A Note About Batters

- Batters must be ice cold. It's the ice-cold batter in contrast to the hot oil that helps create a crisp batter.

- For a heavier, richer-tasting batter, add 1 egg.

- For a puffier batter, add ½ teaspoon baking powder, or 1 egg white beaten until stiff.

- For a finer-textured batter, replace up to half the amount of all-purpose flour with cornstarch or rice flour.

- For flavored batters, use one or more of the following: 2 tablespoons chopped herbs, minced ginger, minced garlic, crushed red chile, your favorite chile sauce, freshly ground black or white pepper, freshly grated nutmeg, powdered mustard, grated citrus zest.

- The following liquids can all be used interchangeably: water, carbonated water, soda water, and beer.

- It's good for the batter to have lumps. The lumps "explode" during cooking and give the batter a "feathery" appearance.

- The batter should barely stick to the vegetables. Depending on the consistency of the batter, adjust by stirring in a little flour or liquid.

All-Purpose Tempura Batter: Combine 1 cup frozen, unbleached all-purpose white flour, ½ teaspoon salt, and 1¼ cups ice-cold carbonated water. Stir briefly, leaving lumps. Place the bowl in a larger bowl containing water and ice. Use immediately.

Tempura Batter with Egg and Baking Soda: To the above mixture, add ¼ teaspoon baking soda to the flour-salt mixture. Stir 1 well-beaten egg into the carbonated water, then combine with the flour mixture as described in the previous batter recipe.

Egg Batter: Dip vegetables in a bowl containing 3 beaten eggs, then into a mixture of 1 cup unbleached all-purpose white flour and 1 teaspoon salt. Then transfer the vegetables to a wire rack. The battered vegetables can be stored on the rack, refrigerated, up to 2 hours before frying.

Beer Batter: Combine 1⅓ cups unbleached all-purpose white flour, 1 teaspoon salt, and ¼ teaspoon powdered white pepper. Stir in 1 tablespoon flavorless cooking oil, 2 well-beaten eggs, and enough beer so the batter barely coats the vegetables, about 1 cup. Stir until most of the lumps disappear. This batter can be refrigerated up to 12 hours before using.

Microwaving and Pressure-Cooking

A detailed explanation of microwaving and pressure-cooking lies beyond the scope of this book. What's common to both these techniques is the ability to dramatically reduce the cooking times of food. Microwaving is a good technique for quickly cooking vegetables, whether whole or cut into pieces. Corn cooks in seconds, artichokes in minutes, and wilted spinach is accomplished without any of the mess found when using a sauté pan. Because the vegetables cook so quickly, they are more nutritious than steamed or poached vegetables. However, perhaps because of long-held cooking habits, I'd rather set up the Chinese steamer. The vegetables' cooking progress is easier to monitor, and the culinary activity is more leisurely and sensual.

PRESSURE COOKER

As for pressure-cooking, I remember childhood days when my twin and I retreated from the stove as a scary whistling came from our mother's aluminum pressure cooker. Those days have thankfully disappeared, and I have enjoyed very good dishes completed in modern stainless-steel pressure cookers. This technique is wonderful for cooking green beans, artichokes, ratatouille, and risotto, and for stocks and soups. The Mercedes-Benz of pressure cookers is the Duromatic, made by the Swiss company Kuhn-Rikon. This is sold with a very good instruction book, which will show you how to adapt traditional recipes, such as those appearing in this book, to cooking in the pressure cooker.

Vegetable Stocks

Many of the recipes in this book call for "vegetable stock." We used a store-bought vegetable "broth" for testing these recipes, and we found its flavor quite acceptable. For a richer flavor, substitute a store-bought or homemade chicken stock, or make your own vegetable stock. Homemade vegetable stocks are easy to make and have a fresher vegetable flavor than their canned cousins.

Vegetable stocks taste best when made with a variety of vegetables. If you are using the stock in a dish that highlights a certain vegetable, then add more of that vegetable to the stock to accent that flavor. Once the stock is made, if you want a stronger flavor, then boil the stock rapidly until it achieves the concentrated flavor you desire. For a more intense flavor, brown the vegetables in a little oil before adding water, or roast the vegetables until brown in a shallow pot in a 400° oven, then add the water, and simmer on the stovetop.

Because vegetables from the cabbage family, including kale, Brussels sprouts, broccoli, and cauliflower, have such strong flavor, don't use them for stocks. Also avoid turnips, rutabagas, beets (unless making beet soup), artichoke trimmings, and onion skins (they make the broth bitter). Add no more than 3 stalks celery, 1 sweet bell pepper, or a handful of fresh herbs (one or any combination of thyme, oregano, parsley). Their flavors can overwhelm a stock. Lastly, never choose any vegetables that are no longer fresh enough to be eaten on their own.

Vegetable Stock

Makes 3 quarts

INGREDIENTS

- ¾ pound carrots, scrubbed
- 1 yellow onion, peeled
- 4 whole green onions, washed
- 1 leek, white and light green parts
- ½ pound button mushrooms
- 2 celery ribs
- 1 cup parsley sprigs
- 1 bay leaf
- 4 sprigs thyme or oregano
- 4 cloves garlic, crushed
- 10 thin slices ginger root
- 4 quarts cold water

PREPARATION

Cut carrots into ½-inch lengths. Chop yellow onion and green onions. Cut the leek lengthwise, separate and wash the layers, then cut the leek crosswise in ¼-inch-wide pieces. Slice the mushrooms and celery. Place all the vegetables and the remaining ingredients in a large pot, and add enough water to cover the vegetables, about 4 quarts. Bring the water to a boil, reduce the heat to low, and simmer the vegetables for 1½ hours. Then, strain, cool to room temperature, and refrigerate. Vegetable stock will keep, refrigerated, for up to 4 days, or frozen, indefinitely.

I am always surprised how easy it is to separate an uncooked artichoke heart and stem from the tough leaves and thistle. Using your fingers and applying a little pressure, just pull off the dark outer leaves and the lighter-colored interior ones. To remove the thistle, lay the artichoke on its side, and with a paring knife cut around the thistle while rotating the artichoke after every cut. It should take no longer than five minutes to trim each artichoke. In this recipe the tart can be assembled hours in advance and then baked in the oven while your guests enjoy appetizers. This is one of the few time-consuming recipes in the book, taking about 1¹/₂ hours to prepare. As a possible menu, accompany this dish with spinach and walnut salad and mango ice cream with chocolate sauce for dessert.

Artichoke and Roasted Red Pepper Tart

Serves 4 as an entrée

INGREDIENTS

1 tart shell (see page 69)

1 egg white

4 medium artichokes

4 red bell peppers

1 whole green onion, minced

3 tablespoons chopped basil leaves

1 large clove garlic, finely minced

3 eggs

1 cup cream

2 tablespoons chopped tarragon leaves

2 teaspoons freshly grated nutmeg

¾ teaspoon salt

½ teaspoon Asian chile sauce

1 cup grated sharp white Cheddar or other sharp firm cheese

½ cup chopped parsley

ADVANCE PREPARATION

Prepare the pie dough and fit it in a 10-inch tart pan. Brush the inside surface with an egg white. Using your fingers, pull off the artichoke leaves. Then using a paring knife, cut out the thistle. Cut the end off each stem. Bring 2 quarts of water to a simmer, add the hearts, and simmer until just tender when pierced with a fork, about 12 minutes. Immediately transfer to a bowl filled with ice and cold water. When chilled, stand each heart with the stem pointing up, and slice through the stems into ¼-inch-wide slices.

Roast the peppers over high gas flames until they are blackened on all sides, or roast them in an electric oven by placing the peppers about 5 inches from the broiler coil. When blackened, transfer the peppers to a paper or plastic bag and tightly close. After 5 minutes, using your fingers, rub off the charred skin. Stem, seed, and cut the peppers into pieces ½ inch wide and 2 inches long. Shred a few tablespoons to use as a garnish.

Prepare the green onion, basil, and garlic. Using a whisk, beat the eggs well. Beat in the cream. Then stir in the green onion, basil, garlic, tarragon, nutmeg, salt, and chile sauce. Grate the cheese and chop the parsley. Then, stir half of these into the mixture.

Set aside the most perfectly cut artichoke slices. Place a layer of artichokes across the tart. Add all the roast pepper in a layer, except the garnish. Add enough of the cream mixture so that it nearly covers the peppers. Cover the peppers with a layer of perfectly cut artichoke slices. Pour in the cream mixture until it just rises to the top edges of the tart. Sprinkle with remaining cheese and parsley, and place the shredded red pepper in the center. *All advance preparation steps may be completed up to 6 hours before you begin the final steps.*

FINAL STEPS

Preheat the oven to 350°. Place the tart on a baking sheet. Put the sheet in the preheated oven, and cook until the tart begins to bubble on the top and lightly browns, about 40 minutes. Remove the tart from the oven, and let cool for 10 minutes. Then slice the tart and serve at once.

The beauties of artichokes, part of the thistle family, are many. Their sweet, grassy taste lingers long after the last bite. Their dramatic cone shape looks both exotic and amusing. And no one eats an artichoke fast. The very effort to pull off leaves, scrape soft flesh between teeth, and the delicate operation to free the tender heart from its thistle crown is part of a slow, almost contemplative process perfectly conducive for lengthy conversation. Always buy artichokes whose leaves are tightly bunched and have no signs of brown spots. We prefer to steam artichokes, which results in artichokes that have more flavor and a better texture than their boiled counterparts. Here are two flavor-intense dips that complement the flavor of artichokes marvelously. As a possible menu, accompany this dish with a gazpacho soup, followed by a heirloom tomato salad and a simple dessert.

Steamed Artichokes with Spicy Asian Dipping Sauces

Serves 4 as a first course or as a side dish

INGREDIENTS
Juice of 1 lemon
4 medium artichokes

ASIAN-CAJUN DIPPING SAUCE
1 cup mayonnaise
1 tablespoon Grand Marnier
1 tablespoon freshly squeezed lime juice
2 teaspoons Worcestershire sauce
1 teaspoon Asian chile sauce
1 tablespoon finely minced fresh ginger
1 teaspoon grated or finely minced orange skin
2 tablespoons chopped cilantro sprigs
½ teaspoon salt

SPICY ASIAN BUTTER SAUCE
½ pound unsalted butter
2 tablespoons thin soy sauce
2 tablespoons freshly squeezed lime juice
1 tablespoon Asian chile sauce
3 cloves garlic, finely minced
2 tablespoons finely minced ginger
¼ cup chopped cilantro sprigs

ADVANCE PREPARATION
Fill a large bowl with cold water; add the juice from 1 lemon. Remove the tough outer leaves of the artichokes. Cut off about ½ inch from the top of each artichoke. Using scissors, snip away the thorns. Trim away the bottom of each stem. As the artichokes are trimmed, place them in the bowl of cold water. Combine the ingredients for the dipping sauce in a bowl, stir well to evenly combine them, and refrigerate. In a small saucepan, combine all the ingredients for the butter sauce.
All advance preparation and cooking steps may be completed up to 8 hours before assembling this dish.

FINAL STEPS
Bring 6 inches of water to a vigorous boil in an Asian steamer or a large pasta pot. Add the artichokes upside down (stems pointing upwards). Cover the pot. Artichokes are done when a skewer will pierce the stem and heart easily, and the leaves pull off easily. Cooking time should be about 30 to 40 minutes. If necessary, add more boiling water to the pot during steaming. Place the saucepan holding the butter sauce over very low heat. Stir the butter until melted, and then remove the butter sauce from the heat. Place the artichokes on plates and serve with the dips.

'm often asked by students what size asparagus is best to buy. Everyone has varying opinions on this matter. I like pencil-thin asparagus for stir-frying, medium to thick asparagus when chilled as an appetizer, and jumbo asparagus hot off the grill. When you bring asparagus home, before refrigerating, if you cut the ends off and stand the asparagus with the stem bottoms submerged in cold water, the asparagus will stay fresher longer. You'll notice, in this recipe, I don't peel the asparagus. Peeling the tougher, lower asparagus spears does make it possible to use more of the asparagus, but for me, I'd rather not bother with it. As a possible menu, accompany this dish with barbecued salmon steaks with saffron orzo and double chocolate brownies with ice cream.

Asparagus Salad with Pine Nuts

Serves 4 to 6 as a salad course or 2 as an entrée

INGREDIENTS

2 bunches asparagus

½ cup raw pine nuts

3 tablespoons flavorless cooking oil

3 cloves garlic, finely minced

¼ cup freshly squeezed orange juice

3 tablespoons thin soy sauce

2 tablespoons Japanese rice vinegar, unseasoned

2 tablespoons brown sugar

1 tablespoon dark sesame oil

1 teaspoon Asian chile sauce

2 tablespoons chopped cilantro sprigs

1 tablespoon white sesame seeds

ADVANCE PREPARATION

Preheat the oven to 325°. Snap the ends off the asparagus. Bring 4 quarts of water to a boil. Add the asparagus and stir. When the asparagus turns a bright green, about 15 to 30 seconds, taste it. It should be crisp but cooked. Immediately transfer the asparagus to a bowl filled with water and ice. When the asparagus is thoroughly chilled, pat it dry with paper towels, and refrigerate. Place the nuts on a cookie sheet and toast them in the preheated oven until golden, about 8 minutes. Set aside. Place the flavorless cooking oil and garlic in a small sauté pan. Combine the orange juice, soy sauce, vinegar, sugar, sesame oil, and chile sauce. Place the sauté pan over medium heat, and when the garlic sizzles, but before it browns, add the orange juice mixture.

Bring the mixture to a low boil, then immediately transfer it to a small bowl. Cool it to room temperature, then stir in the cilantro and refrigerate. Place the sesame seeds in a small ungreased sauté pan and toast them until golden. *All advance preparation steps may be completed up to 8 hours before you begin the final steps.*

FINAL STEPS

Place the asparagus and pine nuts in a large bowl. Stir the salad dressing, then pour over the asparagus. Toss the asparagus until evenly coated with the dressing. Transfer the asparagus to a salad bowl, platter, or individual plates. Sprinkle with sesame seeds. Serve.

e have served this dish many times as a first course, but it also makes an excellent main entrée. The challenge is finding good wrappers. Unfortunately, the frozen mu shu wrappers sold at Asian markets have an unpleasant tough, dry texture. Since many new brands are being introduced (available only in the freezer section of Asian markets), you might experiment with the various brands prior to the dinner. Or, unless you make your own, substitute fresh flour tortillas. If the dinner is very informal, rather than reheating the tortillas in the oven, we enlist the aid of our guests to heat the tortillas by cooking them briefly on both sides placed directly on the gas stove-top flames. The tortillas become piping hot within seconds and acquire a nice charred taste. This recipe is also delicious with broccoli substituted for the asparagus. As a possible menu, accompany this dish with corn soup, endive and tropical fruit salad, and crème brûlée.

Asparagus Mu Shu with Shiitake Mushrooms

Serves 4 to 8 as a first course or 2 as an entrée

INGREDIENTS

2 bunches thin asparagus

¼ pound fresh shiitake mushrooms

3 eggs

1 tablespoon finely minced ginger

2 cloves garlic, finely minced

3 tablespoons Chinese rice wine or
**   dry sherry**

2 tablespoons oyster sauce

1 tablespoon dark sesame oil

1 teaspoon cornstarch

¼ teaspoon freshly ground black pepper

1 cup hoisin sauce

12 mu shu wrappers or flour tortillas

3 tablespoons flavorless cooking oil

ADVANCE PREPARATION

Snap off and discard the asparagus bottoms. If the asparagus is thin to medium, cut the asparagus on a sharp diagonal into 2-inch lengths. If the asparagus is thick, cut the asparagus on a sharp diagonal into 2-inch lengths; after every cut, roll the asparagus one-quarter turn towards you. Cut the asparagus again on a sharp diagonal, repeating the rolling and cutting process.

Cut off and discard the shiitake stems. Overlap the caps and cut them into ¼-inch-wide slices. Combine the asparagus and mushrooms and refrigerate. Beat the eggs and refrigerate. Combine the ginger and garlic. In a small bowl, combine the rice wine, oyster sauce, sesame oil, cornstarch, and black pepper, and refrigerate. In a small bowl, set aside the hoisin sauce. *All advance preparation steps may be completed up to 8 hours before you begin the final steps.*

FINAL STEPS

Preheat the oven to 325°. Stack the mu shu wrappers or tortillas, and wrap them with aluminum foil. Warm the wrappers in the oven for 15 to 20 minutes.

Place a 14- to 16-inch flat-bottom wok or a 12-inch sauté pan over highest heat. When the pan becomes hot, add half the cooking oil. Roll the oil around the wok. When the oil just begins to give off a wisp of smoke, add the eggs. Lightly scramble the eggs, then tip them onto a plate.

Return the wok to highest heat. Add the remaining oil. Add the ginger and garlic, and sauté for 10 seconds. Add the asparagus and mushrooms. Stir and toss until the asparagus become brightly colored, about 2 minutes. Add the rice wine–oyster sauce mixture, and return the eggs to the wok. As soon as the sauce thickens enough to glaze the vegetables and egg, transfer the food to a heated serving platter or dinner plates. Accompany with hot wrappers and hoisin sauce. Each person spreads a little hoisin sauce on their wrapper, adds the mu shu mixture. Each person spreads a little hoisin sauce on their wrapper and adds the mu shu mixture. Roll into a cylinder, turn one end over, and eat using your hands.

Beans: Fresh Fava Beans, Lima Beans, and Soybeans

Farmers' markets in the summer are the place to find fresh fava beans, lima beans, and soybeans. Sold in the pods, they require shelling and simmering in water until tender. Try adding these beans blanched to any of the salads in this book, or serving them either hot or cold tossed with any of the salad dressings, or sauté them raw in extra virgin olive oil with garlic, chopped basil, and tomatoes, and cook until tender. Your dinner guests will be instant fans of these fresh beans added raw to, or as a replacement for, the peppers on page 76, or blanched and added to either of the broccoli stir-fry recipes, pages 31-33.

Fava Beans: Native to the Mediterranean, where it has been cultivated since Stone Age times, the fava bean has also been grown in China for at least 2000 years. Fava beans are sold in large dark-green pods and must be very fresh if they are to be tender. Avoid buying large, bulging pods, which indicate the beans are too mature. Very young fava beans just need to be blanched briefly before they are used in salads, or can be sautéed raw. Older fava beans must be peeled before cooking. Using your thumbnail or a paring knife, split the outer skin of each fava bean and discard the outer skin. Store raw beans in the shell, refrigerated, up to 4 days. Shelled fava beans will take only a few minutes to poach if young or as long as 15 minutes if mature.

Lima Beans: Discovered by the Europeans in Lima, Peru, in the 1500s, these kidney-shaped beans, sold in their dark-green pods, are available fresh from June through September. The two common varieties are Baby limas and the large Fordhook limas, which have a fuller flavor than the Baby variety. Both varieties have a thinner skin than fava beans. Store them in the shell, refrigerated, up to 4 days. Three pounds of limas in their pods will serve 4 people. Shell the day you plan to cook them. Simmer covered until tender, about 10 minutes.

Soybeans: Cultivated for thousands of years by the Chinese, soybeans were introduced to Japan in the sixth century, Europe in the seventeenth century, and were not grown in the United States until the 1920s. Now we produce one-third of the total world production. Soybeans are supremely nutritious, being high in protein and desirable oils, and low in carbohydrates. More than one thousand varieties exist, ranging from the size of a pea to a cherry. The pods are tan to black, with each pod containing 2 to 4 soybeans. Fresh soybeans can be blanched, boiled, or sautéed, just the way one cooks fava and lima beans. Store soybeans in the pods, refrigerated, up to 4 days. One pound of pods will yield about 1½ cups of shelled soybeans. Simmer covered until tender, about 10 minutes.

This recipe is based on a salad I have enjoyed many times, created by Brian Streeter, long-time winery chef at Cakebread Cellars. The key technique is to roast the beets, which concentrates their flavor and heightens their sweetness. The salad is a little time-consuming to prepare, although the preparation can be done hours in advance of serving. Don't tell a single guest that beets will make their appearance. Just dim the dining lights and observe even the most finicky eaters speedily finishing their salad. As a possible menu, accompany this dish with a mushroom soup, sesame seed biscuits, and Mexican flan.

Roasted Beet Salad with Fresh Mozzarella Cheese

Serves 4 to 6 as a salad course or 2 as an entrée

INGREDIENTS

3 bunches (about 18) small beets, red, golden, or a mixture of the two

1 cup sliced almonds, or ½ cup pine nuts

3 ounces buffalo mozzarella cheese or soft goat cheese

4 cups baby spinach leaves, arugula, or baby lettuce greens

DRESSING

⅓ cup extra virgin olive oil

3 tablespoons freshly squeezed lemon juice

1 tablespoon thin soy sauce

¼ teaspoon freshly ground black pepper

2 tablespoons chopped basil leaves

1 clove garlic, finely minced

ADVANCE PREPARATION

Preheat the oven to 400°. Trim the tops off the beets and reserve for another dish. Scrub the beets, and then wrap them in aluminum foil. Place them on a baking sheet and roast in the preheated oven about 30 minutes, until they can be easily pierced with a knife. Remove the beets from the oven. When they are cool enough to handle, peel away the skins. Cut the beets into thin slices and refrigerate. Reduce the oven temperature to 325°; then toast the nuts until light golden, about 8 minutes. Set aside nuts. Thinly slice the mozzarella or crumble the goat cheese; then refrigerate. Keep the spinach in the refrigerator. In a small container, combine all ingredients for the salad dressing. *All advance preparation steps may be completed up to 8 hours before you begin the final steps.*

FINAL STEPS

Place the spinach or greens in a bowl. Stir the dressing, then pour half the dressing over the spinach and toss until evenly coated with the dressing. Place the spinach on salad plates. If using mozzarella, add the slices next, then the beets, and a sprinkling of nuts. If using goat cheese, add the beets first, on top of the spinach, then add the goat cheese, and nuts. Sprinkle on the remaining dressing and serve at once.

Bok choy has over twenty different varieties, each having a charming name such as "horse's tail," "horse's ear," and "spoon spoon." It is the most popular of the hundreds of varieties of cabbages used by the Chinese. Baby bok choy, about 6 inches long, is often water-blanched until the color brightens and then stir-fried whole with mushrooms and oyster sauce. We prefer to separate the stems, since it is not always possible to wash sand out from the interior layers. Substitute another type of cabbage or summer squash if the stems are no longer rigid or the leaves have yellow spots. As a possible menu, accompany this dish with chilled barbecued chicken rubbed with herbs, Asian noodles, and a hot fudge sundae.

Stir-Fried Bok Choy with Mushrooms and Peppers

Serves 4 as a side dish

INGREDIENTS

6 baby bok choy, or ½ large bok choy

1 small red bell pepper

½ pound medium button mushrooms

2 tablespoons finely minced ginger

2 tablespoons flavorless cooking oil

SAUCE

3 tablespoons chopped basil or mint leaves

⅓ cup unsweetened coconut milk

3 tablespoons Chinese rice wine or dry sherry

1 tablespoon oyster sauce

2 teaspoons hoisin sauce

2 teaspoons dark sesame oil

2 teaspoons cornstarch

1 teaspoon curry powder

½ teaspoon sugar

ADVANCE PREPARATION

If using baby bok choy, cut each stalk in half on a sharp diagonal. If using mature bok choy, cut each stalk on a sharp diagonal into 1- to 2-inch-long pieces, each about ¼ inch wide. Cut the leaves in quarters. Stem, seed, and cut the pepper into pieces 1 to 2 inches long and ½ inch wide. Cut each mushroom into 4 thin slices. Combine all the vegetables. You should have 4 to 5 cups of vegetables; refrigerate. Combine the ginger and cooking oil. In a bowl, combine the sauce ingredients, stir, and then refrigerate. *All advance preparation steps may be completed up to 8 hours before you begin the final steps.*

FINAL STEPS

Place a 14- to 16-inch flat-bottom wok or 12-inch sauté pan over highest heat. When the wok becomes very hot, add the cooking oil to the center. Roll the oil around the wok, and when the oil gives off a wisp of smoke, add the vegetables. Stir and toss the vegetables until the bok choy leaves turn bright green. Stir the sauce, then pour the sauce into the wok. Stir and toss the vegetables until the sauce thickens and evenly coats all the vegetables, about 30 seconds. Immediately transfer to a heated serving platter or dinner plates and serve at once.

In this stir-fry dish, the intense color, flavor, and texture of broccoli is in dramatic contrast to the cubes of bean curd and thinly sliced shiitake mushrooms. At the very end of the cooking process, a beaten egg is mixed into the vegetables in order to thicken the sauce and create a richer-tasting dish. For variation, in place of broccoli, substitute asparagus cut on a sharp diagonal into 1-inch lengths, or zucchini cut in half lengthwise and then cut crosswise on a sharp diagonal in 1/8-inch-wide slices. As a possible menu, accompany this dish with steamed jasmine rice and caramel pineapple cake.

Broccoli with Tofu and Shiitake Mushrooms

Serves 2 to 4 as a side dish

INGREDIENTS

1 large broccoli head, about
    1 pound
4 fresh shiitake mushrooms
3 whole green onions
6 ounces firm bean curd
4 cloves garlic, finely minced
2 tablespoons finely minced ginger
1 egg
1 tablespoon cornstarch
2 tablespoons flavorless cooking oil

SAUCE

1/2 cup vegetable or chicken broth
2 tablespoons thin soy sauce
1 tablespoon dark sesame oil
2 teaspoons hoisin sauce
1/2 teaspoon Asian chile sauce

ADVANCE PREPARATION

Trim tough stem ends from broccoli and peel stems with a vegetable peeler. Cut stems on a sharp diagonal in 1/8-inch-thick slices. Separate the broccoli florets. You should have approximately 4 cups of broccoli. Discard the mushroom stems, and cut the caps into 1/4-inch-wide slices. Discard the root ends from the green onions, and then cut the green onions on a sharp diagonal into 1-inch lengths. Cut the bean curd into 1/2-inch cubes. Combine the broccoli, mushrooms, green onions, bean curd, garlic, and ginger; refrigerate. In a small bowl, beat the egg and refrigerate. Set aside the cornstarch and cooking oil. In a small bowl, combine all the sauce ingredients, and refrigerate. *All advance preparation steps may be completed up to 8 hours before you begin the final steps.*

FINAL STEPS

Mix the cornstarch with an equal amount of cold water. Place a 14- to 16-inch flat-bottom wok or a 12-inch sauté pan over highest heat. When the wok becomes very hot, add the cooking oil to the center. Roll the oil around the wok, and when the oil gives off a wisp of smoke, add the vegetables. Stir and toss for 30 seconds; then add the sauce. Immediately cover the wok. Let the broccoli steam for 20 seconds, then remove the wok top and stir-fry for a few seconds. If the broccoli has not turned a bright green, cover and repeat the steaming process. As soon as the broccoli turns bright green, stir in enough of the cornstarch mixture so that the sauce thickens slightly. Stir in the egg. As soon as the egg cooks, about 5 seconds, transfer the broccoli to a heated serving platter or dinner plates and serve at once.

se every part of the broccoli head. Cut off the florets, keeping each little stem attached. If you are planning to sauté or stir-fry the florets, using a paring knife, make a few cuts down the length of each stem. In this way the florets and their attached stems cook evenly. The thick bottom stem, with its firm texture and more subtle flavor, is the best part of the broccoli. With a vegetable peeler, remove and discard the outer stringy layer. Then cut the stem into the desired shape. In this recipe, to speed the cooking of the broccoli, the broccoli is stir-fried briefly, and then the sauce is added and the broccoli is steam-cooked with the wok covered. As a possible menu, accompany this dish with rice with chives, and pears poached in Cabernet Sauvignon.

Wok-Seared Broccoli with Orange Sauce and Pine Nuts

Serves 2 to 4 as a side dish

INGREDIENTS

½ **cup pine nuts**

1 **large broccoli head, about 1 pound**

3 **whole green onions**

3 **cloves garlic, finely minced**

2 **tablespoons flavorless cooking oil**

ORANGE SAUCE

½ **teaspoon grated orange skin**

⅓ **cup freshly squeezed orange juice**

½ **cup Chinese rice wine or dry sherry**

1 **tablespoon oyster sauce**

1 **teaspoon cornstarch**

½ **teaspoon sugar**

¼ **teaspoon Asian chile sauce**

ADVANCE PREPARATION

Preheat the oven to 325° to toast the nuts. Cut the stems from the florets, then trim off tough stem ends and peel the stems with a vegetable peeler. Cut the stems on a sharp diagonal into ⅛-inch-thick slices. Separate the broccoli florets. You should have approximately 4 cups of broccoli. Discard the root ends from the green onions and then cut the green onions on a sharp diagonal into 1-inch lengths. Combine the broccoli and green onions and refrigerate. Toast the pine nuts in the preheated oven until golden, about 8 minutes; then set them aside in a bowl. Set aside the garlic. Set aside the cooking oil. In a small bowl, combine all the sauce ingredients; refrigerate. *All advance preparation steps may be completed up to 8 hours before you begin the final steps.*

FINAL STEPS

Place a 14- to 16-inch flat-bottom wok or a 12-inch sauté pan over highest heat. When the wok becomes very hot, add the cooking oil to the center. Roll the oil around the wok, and when the oil gives off a wisp of smoke, add the vegetables and garlic. Stir and toss for 30 seconds, then add the sauce. Immediately cover the wok. Let the broccoli steam for 20 seconds, then remove the cover and stir-fry for a few seconds. If the broccoli has not turned a bright green, cover the wok and repeat the steaming process. As soon as the broccoli turns bright green, stir in the nuts. Immediately transfer to a heated serving platter or dinner plates and serve at once.

I was astounded the first time I saw how Brussels sprouts, those flavorful little heads of cabbages, "pop out" everywhere along a long single stalk. It is a bizarre, almost magical sight. First grown in the sixteenth century in Belgium, they can be boiled, steamed, blanched, placed on skewers for barbecuing, or stir-fried. For variation, in place of Brussels sprouts in this recipe, substitute broccoli separated into individual flowers, or asparagus cut on a sharp diagonal into 1-inch lengths. As a possible menu, accompany this dish with cracked crab, garlic bread, and fresh berries for dessert.

Brussels Sprouts with Asian Hollandaise Sauce

Serves 2 to 4 as a side dish

INGREDIENTS

1 pound Brussels sprouts

3 large egg yolks

2 tablespoons freshly squeezed lemon juice

8 tablespoons unsalted butter

¼ teaspoon salt

¼ teaspoon Asian chile sauce

2 teaspoons finely minced ginger

1 teaspoon grated or finely minced lemon peel

½ teaspoon freshly grated nutmeg

ADVANCE PREPARATION

Trim off the tough outer leaves from the Brussels sprouts; then cut each piece in half. In separate containers, set aside the egg yolks and 1 tablespoon of the lemon juice; refrigerate. Set aside 1 tablespoon unsalted butter and bring it to room temperature. Cut the remaining butter into small pieces and set aside in a microwave-safe bowl. In a small bowl, combine the remaining 1 tablespoon lemon juice with the salt, chile sauce, ginger, and grated lemon peel; refrigerate. Set aside nutmeg to grate. *All advance preparation steps may be completed up to 8 hours before you begin the final steps.*

FINAL STEPS

Bring water to a boil in a Chinese steamer, or pour 1 inch of water in a 4-quart saucepan with a collapsible stainless-steel vegetable steamer. When the water boils, add the Brussels sprouts, cover the steamer, and cook until the Brussels sprouts are tender when pierced with a fork, about 6 to 8 minutes. Transfer to heated dinner plates.

Melt the 7 tablespoons of butter in a microwave oven. Place 1 quart of water in a 2-quart saucepan and bring to a boil; then reduce the heat and maintain the water at a simmer. In a very small saucepan, beat the egg yolks with the 1 tablespoon lemon juice. Add the tablespoon of room-temperature butter. Place the small saucepan inside the larger saucepan holding the simmering water. Beat the yolks with a whisk until the sauce thickens to the consistency of heavy cream. Immediately turn off the heat, and slowly beat in the melted butter. Stir in the ginger–lemon juice mixture. The hollandaise sauce takes about 2 minutes to make. If the Brussels sprouts are not done, keep the small saucepan holding the hollandaise sauce inside the larger saucepan, with the heat off. If the hollandaise sauce is too thick to pour, stir in a little water to thin the consistency of the sauce.

Spoon the hollandaise sauce over the Brussels sprouts. Using a nutmeg grater or the fine mesh of a cheese grater, grate a dusting of nutmeg over the hollandaise sauce. Serve at once.

This is a rich-tasting dish that makes a great work-night main entrée. Choose either the common white-head cabbage or the very attractive savoy cabbage. The latter have beautiful open heads whose leaves range in color from white with green edging to bright red or various shades of green. Choose small heads with crisp leaves and no signs of brown. The special flavor in this dish comes from using salted, fermented Chinese black beans. These are completely different than dried or canned black beans, and are usually sold only at Chinese markets. We find the Chinese black bean "pastes" or "sauces" overly salty and prefer the salted black beans sold in 17-ounce yellow cardboard canisters, labeled "Yang Jiang Preserved Beans." As a possible menu, accompany this dish with a tomato and basil salad, steamed jasmine rice, and ginger ice cream.

Cabbage with Eggs, Chinese Black Beans, and Chiles — *Serves 4 to 6 as a first course or 2 as an entrée*

INGREDIENTS

¼ **head green cabbage or savoy cabbage**

4 **fresh shiitake mushrooms**

3 **whole green onions**

2 **eggs**

3 **tablespoons flavorless cooking oil**

3 **cloves garlic, finely minced**

1 **tablespoon Chinese salted black beans**

1 **tablespoon unsalted butter, room temperature**

SAUCE

3 **tablespoons vegetable or chicken broth**

1 **tablespoon dark sesame oil**

1 **tablespoon thin soy sauce**

1 **teaspoon cornstarch**

½ **teaspoon sugar**

½ **teaspoon Asian chile sauce**

ADVANCE PREPARATION

Cut the cabbage into ⅛-inch-wide slices, then cut slices lengthwise into 2-inch pieces. You will need 3 cups. Discard the mushroom stems, then cut the caps into ⅛-inch-wide slices. Cut the green onions on a sharp diagonal in ⅛-inch-wide pieces. Combine the vegetables and refrigerate. Beat the eggs well and refrigerate. Reserve half the cooking oil. Combine the remaining cooking oil with the garlic. Rinse and then mince the black beans. Then add the black beans to the oil-garlic mixture. Set aside the butter. In a small bowl, combine all the sauce ingredients; refrigerate. *All advance preparation steps may be completed up to 8 hours before you begin the final steps.*

FINAL STEPS

Place a 14- or 16-inch flat-bottom wok or a 12-inch sauté pan over very high heat. When it is very hot, add the cooking oil (not the oil containing garlic and black beans). Roll the oil around the sides of the wok. When the oil becomes hot and just gives off a wisp of smoke, add the eggs. Scramble the eggs and then set them aside.

Immediately return the wok to highest heat. Add the oil-garlic mixture. Roll the oil around the wok. When the garlic begins to sizzle, add the vegetables. Stir and toss until the cabbage brightens in color, about 2 minutes. Immediately add the sauce and return the eggs to the wok. Stir and toss briefly. Add the room-temperature butter. Stir until everything is evenly combined. Transfer to a heated serving dish or dinner plates. Serve at once.

Great risotto depends on several factors. Use only arborio rice, which absorbs large amounts of flavorful liquid while retaining a marvelously firm texture. Beretta is the brand stocked by most American supermarkets, though the Campanini brand sold at Italian markets is superior. Rather than trying to precook the risotto, which some chefs recommend, cook the risotto at the last moment and stir the rice frequently. The instant the rice no longer has a raw texture but still is firm, it should be served. The idea for carrot risotto came from our cooking friend John Ash. If you want a more intense carrot taste, he recommends cooking the rice with 1 cup shredded carrots, or stirring ¼ cup of fresh carrot juice into the risotto towards the end of cooking. As a possible menu, accompany this dish with blue cheese and watercress salad, and an apple tart.

Carrot Risotto

Serves 4 as an entrée or 4 to 6 as a side dish

INGREDIENTS

¼ cup unsalted butter or olive oil

2 tablespoons finely minced ginger

3 bunches baby carrots, or 1 bunch medium carrots

6 cups vegetable or chicken broth

¼ cup dry vermouth or white wine

1 teaspoon grated orange zest

½ teaspoon Asian chile sauce

1 cup arborio rice

¼ cup chopped basil leaves

¼ cup chopped parsley

1 cup freshly grated imported Parmesan cheese

Salt and pepper, to taste

ADVANCE PREPARATION

Combine the butter with the ginger and set aside. Remove the stems and peel the carrots. Cut the carrots on a sharp diagonal. Bring 2 quarts of water to a boil, stir in the carrots, and cook until they become tender, about 3 to 5 minutes. Immediately transfer the carrots to a bowl filled with cold water and ice; when chilled, drain and pat the carrots dry; refrigerate. In a saucepan, combine the broth, dry vermouth, grated orange zest, and chile sauce; refrigerate. Set aside the rice. *All advance preparation steps may be completed up to 4 hours before you begin the final steps.*

FINAL STEPS

Chop the herbs. Grate the cheese. Place the saucepan holding the broth over low heat, bring it to a low simmer, and maintain it at this temperature. Place a 3-quart saucepan over medium heat. Add the butter and ginger. Sauté the ginger for 20 seconds. Add the rice, and sauté briefly. Add ⅓ of the broth. Continue stirring occasionally. Every time the liquid disappears, add another ladle of the hot broth. When the rice just tastes tender, after about 20 minutes total cooking time, stir in the carrots. After 2 more minutes, stir in the herbs and cheese. Taste and adjust the seasonings, especially the salt and pepper. Serve at once.

auliflower, which is a member of the cabbage family, derives its name from the Latin **caulis** *("stalk") and* **flores** *("flower"). White cauliflower is sold by supermarkets, but at most farmers' markets, you'll find light-green and purple varieties. However, they lose most of their spectacular pigmentation during cooking. Cauliflower is delicious cooked whole, whether steamed, done in the pressure cooker, or barbecued slowly with the coals scattered around the edges of the grill. It's also great separated into its tiny florets and stir-fried with Chinese sauces, or as done in this recipe, by matching cauliflower and Mediterranean seasonings with an Asian cooking method. As with wok-cooking of broccoli, here the cauliflower is briefly stir-fried and then steam-cooked with the wok covered in order to promote quick, even cooking. As a possible menu, accompany this dish with salmon salad with dill, hot sourdough rolls, and an upside-down pineapple cake.*

Stir-Fried Cauliflower with Mediterranean Accents

Serves 4 as a side dish and 2 as an entrée

INGREDIENTS

½ cup walnut pieces

10 sundried tomato slices

8 kalamata olives or other imported black pitted olives

1 head cauliflower

¼ cup extra virgin olive oil

4 cloves garlic, finely minced

1 shallot, minced

1 cup vegetable or chicken broth

1 lemon

½ teaspoon crushed red chile

½ teaspoon salt

¼ cup chopped basil leaves

ADVANCE PREPARATION

Preheat the oven to 350°. Drop the walnuts in 4 cups of rapidly boiling water. Cook for 3 minutes. Then drain the walnuts, spread them on a baking sheet, and place the sheet in the preheated oven until the walnuts turn dark golden, about 15 minutes. Set nuts aside. Place dried tomato slices in a bowl, cover with boiling water, and soak for 30 minutes; then remove the tomatoes and thinly slice. Chop the olives.

Trim off and discard the cauliflower stem and leaves. Separate the cauliflower into its individual florets. Cut the florets in half or into wedges; then refrigerate. In a small bowl, combine oil, garlic, and shallot. In another bowl, combine broth, the grated zest from 1 lemon, chile, salt, and basil; refrigerate. Into a small bowl, squeeze the lemon, strain the juice, and refrigerate.
All advance preparation steps may be completed up to 8 hours before you begin the final steps.

FINAL STEPS

Place a wok over highest heat. When the wok is very hot, add the oil, garlic, and shallot. Sauté for a few seconds and then add the cauliflower, tomatoes, and olives. Stir and toss for 5 seconds, then add the broth mixture. Immediately cover the wok and steam-cook the cauliflower until it becomes tender when pierced with a fork, about 8 minutes. Periodically during cooking, remove the top and stir the cauliflower. When the cauliflower becomes tender, stir in the nuts and add 1 to 2 tablespoons lemon juice, depending on how lemon-tasting and tart you want the cauliflower to be. Transfer to a heated serving platter or dinner plates. Serve at once.

elery root, or "celeriac," is a variety of celery that is cultivated just for its root. When you buy celery root, press it with your fingers to make sure there are no soft spots, which indicate that it's spoiling. Using a sharp knife, trim off any small roots or knobs, and then carefully cut away all the outer skin, revealing the pure white flesh. To prevent discoloration, transfer the pieces to a bowl of water containing the juice from one lemon. Try cutting celery root into matchstick-shaped pieces and adding it to salads. Cut celery root into cubes or chunks and stir it into stews during the last 10 minutes of simmering. Or rub strips of celery root with olive oil, garlic, salt, and pepper, and then barbecue the pieces. This is one of the easiest recipes in the book. Be sure to simmer the celery root until it is tender, and then cool it to room temperature before puréeing it in an electric blender, so there's no danger of hot liquid erupting from the blender. As a possible menu, accompany this dish with baby lettuce greens with shrimp and papaya, and baked apples with rum sauce.

Celery Root Soup with Ginger and Herbs

Serves 4 to 8 as a side dish

INGREDIENTS

2 tablespoons unsalted butter

2 tablespoons finely minced ginger

2 small shallots, chopped

1 celery root, about 1½ pounds

2¼ cups vegetable or chicken broth

1 cup heavy cream

1 teaspoon freshly grated nutmeg

½ teaspoon salt

¼ teaspoon ground white pepper

¼ cup cilantro sprigs or chives

ADVANCE PREPARATION

In a bowl, combine the butter, ginger, and shallots. Using a knife, trim off and discard all the celery root skin. Cut the celery root into ¼-inch-wide slices; then cut the slices into 1-inch-wide strips. Place a 3-quart saucepan over medium heat. Add the butter, ginger, and shallots. When the ginger sizzles but has not turned brown, about 3 minutes, add the celery root slices and vegetable broth. Bring the broth to a low boil, cover the saucepan, and reduce the heat so the liquid is at a very low boil. Cook the celery root slices until they become tender, about 5 to 7 minutes. Then remove the saucepan from the heat.

When the liquid has cooled to room temperature, purée it in an electric blender, not a food processor. The liquid will be very thick. Pour it through a medium-meshed strainer, working the liquid through the strainer using the back of a spoon. Transfer the liquid back to the 3-quart saucepan. Add the cream, nutmeg, salt, and white pepper. Heat the soup to a simmer and adjust the seasonings, especially for salt and pepper. You should have about 4 cups of soup. If the soup is too thick, thin it with a little vegetable broth. Refrigerate. *All advance preparation steps may be completed up to 4 hours before you begin the final steps.*

FINAL STEPS

Chop the cilantro or chives. Bring the soup to a simmer. Taste and adjust the seasonings. Transfer the soup to a heated soup tureen or soup bowls. Sprinkle on the cilantro or chives, and serve at once.

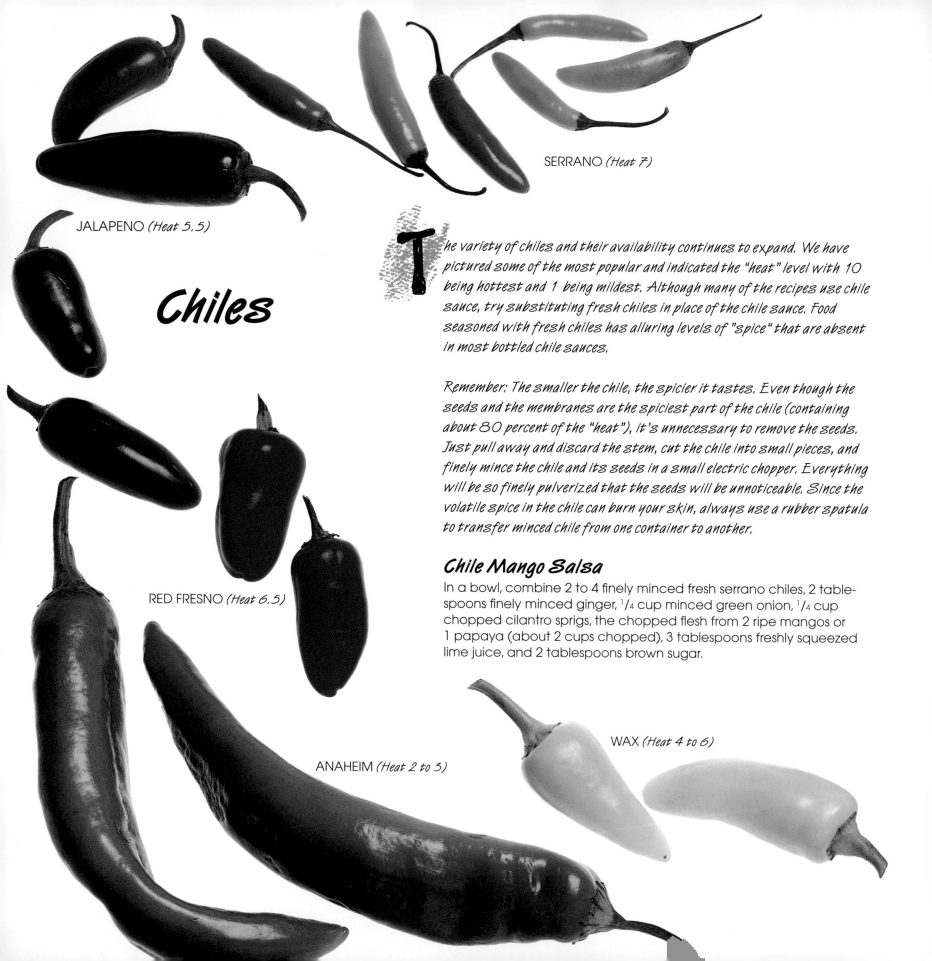

SERRANO *(Heat 7)*

JALAPENO *(Heat 5.5)*

Chiles

The variety of chiles and their availability continues to expand. We have pictured some of the most popular and indicated the "heat" level with 10 being hottest and 1 being mildest. Although many of the recipes use chile sauce, try substituting fresh chiles in place of the chile sauce. Food seasoned with fresh chiles has alluring levels of "spice" that are absent in most bottled chile sauces.

Remember: The smaller the chile, the spicier it tastes. Even though the seeds and the membranes are the spiciest part of the chile (containing about 80 percent of the "heat"), it's unnecessary to remove the seeds. Just pull away and discard the stem, cut the chile into small pieces, and finely mince the chile and its seeds in a small electric chopper. Everything will be so finely pulverized that the seeds will be unnoticeable. Since the volatile spice in the chile can burn your skin, always use a rubber spatula to transfer minced chile from one container to another.

Chile Mango Salsa

In a bowl, combine 2 to 4 finely minced fresh serrano chiles, 2 tablespoons finely minced ginger, $1/4$ cup minced green onion, $1/4$ cup chopped cilantro sprigs, the chopped flesh from 2 ripe mangos or 1 papaya (about 2 cups chopped), 3 tablespoons freshly squeezed lime juice, and 2 tablespoons brown sugar.

RED FRESNO *(Heat 6.5)*

ANAHEIM *(Heat 2 to 3)*

WAX *(Heat 4 to 6)*

THAI *(Heat 7 to 8)*

Rellenos, in Spanish, means "stuffed," and although Mexican restaurants in America stuff the chiles with a bland-tasting cheese mixture, many exciting variations await the creative cook. For example, any Asian seafood dumpling filling works great as a stuffing or, as in this recipe, a mixture of fresh shiitake mushrooms, dried currants, pine nuts, chopped cilantro, and goat cheese. While chiles rellenos can be cooked in a 400° oven for 20 minutes, they taste better when dipped into a batter and shallow-fried. In terms of chiles, we prefer using fresh poblano chiles, which are slightly smaller and have a more complex flavor than fresh Anaheim chiles. But never use canned chiles, whose limp texture will ruin chiles rellenos. As a possible menu, accompany this dish with tortilla soup, watercress salad, and chocolate tile cakes.

Chiles Rellenos

Serves 4 as a side dish and 2 as an entrée

INGREDIENTS

6 fresh poblano chiles or medium-sized fresh Anaheim chiles

1 red bell pepper

¼ cup pine nuts

2 tablespoons olive oil

3 cloves garlic, finely minced

4 ounces fresh shiitake mushrooms

2 whole green onions, minced

¼ cup chopped cilantro sprigs

¼ cup dried currants

4 ounces soft goat cheese

½ teaspoon salt

½ teaspoon Asian chile sauce

3 eggs, well beaten

½ cup unbleached white flour

Chile Mango Salsa, page 40, or one of the salsas on page 99

2 cups flavorless cooking oil

ADVANCE PREPARATION

Place the chiles and the pepper directly over gas stove-top flames turned to high. Char until partially blackened on all sides. Or char under the broiler. When the chiles and pepper are charred, transfer them to a plastic bag, and seal for 10 minutes. Then rub off all the black skin. Make a cut lengthwise along each chile, rinse out the seeds, and pat the chiles dry with paper towels. Stem, seed, and mince the pepper. Preheat the oven to 325° and then toast the pine nuts until golden, about 8 minutes. Combine the oil and garlic. Discard the mushroom stems, then cut the caps into ⅛-inch-wide slices. Heat a 10-inch sauté pan over medium-high heat. When the pan is hot, add the oil and garlic. When the garlic sizzles, add the mushrooms. Cook the mushrooms until they wilt, about 3 minutes, then transfer the mushrooms and garlic to a mixing bowl.

In the bowl containing the mushrooms, add the chopped pepper, pine nuts, green onions, cilantro, currants, goat cheese, salt, and chile sauce. Using your fingers, mix well. Then gently fill the chiles with the stuffing. Refrigerate. Set aside

the beaten eggs and the flour. Prepare the salsa. *All advance preparation steps may be completed up to 8 hours before you begin the final steps.*

FINAL STEPS

If using a salsa, warm it. Dip the chiles in beaten egg, then gently roll them in flour and transfer them to a wire rack. Place a 12- or 14-inch frying pan over medium-high heat. Add the cooking oil. When the cooking oil becomes hot enough so that the end of a wooden spoon when dipped into the oil begins to bubble around the tip (but the oil has not become so hot that it has begun to smoke), gently add the stuffed chiles. Cook the chiles a few at a time, until they are golden on both sides. The total cooking time is about 3 minutes. Transfer the chiles to a wire rack and pat them dry with paper towels. Then transfer the fried chiles to heated dinner plates. Spoon the salsa around the sides of the chiles. Serve at once.

HABANERO *(Heat 10)*

POBLANO *(Heat 3)*

ears ago one of my students taught me a trick to impart a stronger sweet corn flavor to corn soups: simmer the cobs in vegetable stock or water. That's a key element of the glorious taste of this soup. The other element is an ancho-chile "jam" that floats in little lettuce-cup "boats" across the soup's surface. Each diner capsizes their boat and then swirls the ancho-chile jam into the soup. You'll have extra ancho-chile jam. This lasts indefinitely in the refrigerator. Use it as a flavorful spread for hamburgers, in sandwiches, as a pizza sauce, and wherever you want to add a strong taste accent. As a possible menu, accompany this dish with spinach, crab, and mango salad; wild rice; and peach cobbler with ice cream.

Thai Corn Soup with Chile-Jam Accent

Serves 6 or 8 as a first course or 4 as an entrée

INGREDIENTS

10 ears white corn, husked

2 dried ancho chiles

¼ cup plum or currant jelly

2 tablespoons red wine vinegar

1 tablespoon honey

1 tablespoon Asian chile sauce

3 tablespoons flavorless cooking oil

2 tablespoons finely minced ginger

3 cloves garlic, finely minced

Minced zest and juice from 1 lime

3 cups unsweetened coconut milk

3 tablespoons Thai or Vietnamese fish sauce, or 1 teaspoon salt

2 tablespoons cornstarch

½ cup cilantro sprigs

2 large leaves of iceberg lettuce

ADVANCE PREPARATION

Stand the corn on its end and cut off the kernels. You should have about 3 to 4 cups. Refrigerate the kernels. Discard half the cobs. Break the remaining cobs in half, place them in a 3-quart saucepan, add water to cover, and bring to a simmer. Cover and simmer 30 minutes. Then discard the cobs, strain the liquid, and set 3 cups aside. Bring 1 quart of water to a boil. Remove the saucepan from the heat, add the dried chiles, and cover the saucepan. After 30 minutes, rinse the chiles with cold water; then stem and seed the chiles. Place the chiles, jelly, vinegar, honey, and chile sauce in a food processor and process until smooth. Transfer the mixture to a bowl and refrigerate. Combine the oil, ginger, and garlic. Combine the corn broth, the juice of the lime, the zest, coconut milk, fish sauce, and the cornstarch; refrigerate. Set aside the cilantro, and refrigerate it also. Prepare 8 small lettuce cups by cutting circles each about the size of a silver dollar; refrigerate. *All advance preparation steps may be completed up to 8 hours before you begin the final steps.*

FINAL STEPS

Chop the cilantro. Place a 4-quart saucepan over medium-high heat. Add the oil, ginger, and garlic. Sauté for a few seconds. Before the garlic browns, add the corn-coconut broth. Bring to a simmer and add the corn kernels and cilantro. The moment the soup just comes to a low boil, turn off the heat. Taste and adjust the seasonings, especially for salt. Transfer the soup to heated soup bowls. Place a spoonful of chile jam in each lettuce cup. Float the lettuce cup in the soup. Serve at once.

This is a very delicate yet rich and delicious mousse that is perfect for a light lunch or first course. You can either fashion little boats from dried corn husks to steam the mixture in or, alternatively, pour the liquid into buttered ramekins or timbales and bake them surrounded by a water bath. We prefer using the corn husks, but it does require several bamboo or aluminum Chinese steamer tiers to hold the little "boats." As a possible menu, accompany this dish with barbecued shrimp, roasted sweet pepper salad, and lemon ice cream with chocolate sauce.

Corn Tamale Mousse —————————— *Serves 6 as a first course or side dish*

INGREDIENTS

12 dried corn husks

4 to 5 ears white corn, husked

4 large eggs

1 cup heavy cream

2 teaspoons cornstarch

2 teaspoons Asian chile sauce

1 teaspoon salt

1 teaspoon ground cumin

¼ cup chopped cilantro sprigs, plus sprigs for garnish

¼ cup grated imported Parmesan cheese

ADVANCE PREPARATION

Cover the dried corn husks with cold water for 1 hour. Cut enough kernels off the corn cobs to fill 2 cups. Transfer the kernels to a food processor and liquefy. Remove the processor top and add the eggs, cream, cornstarch, chile sauce, salt, and cumin. Process for 15 seconds. Pour the liquid through a medium-meshed strainer, pressing the corn pulp with the back of a rubber spatula. Stir the chopped cilantro and cheese into the strained liquid. You will have 3 cups. Refrigerate. *All advance preparation steps may be completed up to 8 hours before you begin the final steps.*

FINAL STEPS

Bring 4 inches of water to a low boil in a Chinese steamer, or in a steamer that you have improvised by using a large stock pot or roasting pan. Using kitchen string, tie a corn husk at each end and open up the center so that the husk forms a boat. Add about ¼ cup filling to each boat. Place the tamales on the steamer tier or a wire rack, and place the tier over the boiling water. Cover the steamer and cook about 8 minutes, until the filling is thoroughly heated and has puffed up slightly. Garnish with cilantro sprigs. Serve at once.

Alternatively, preheat the oven to 325°. Butter six ½-cup ramekins or timbales. Fill the ramekins with the corn liquid. Place the ramekins in a deep baking dish and add enough hot water so that it rises halfway up the side of the ramekins. Cover the ramekins with cooking paper or foil to stop a crust from forming. Place the baking dish containing the ramekins in the oven. Cook 30 minutes. Remove the ramekins from the water and let them cool for 5 minutes. Run a knife around the sides of the ramekins, then gently invert the custard onto plates. Garnish with cilantro sprigs. Serve at once.

Homemade pickles are so easy to make and so delicious. Choose any firm cucumber, such as pickling cucumbers, Armenian cucumbers, Japanese cucumbers, or hothouse (sometimes sold as "gourmet" or "English") cucumbers. If you want pickles with an extra-firm texture, split the cucumbers in half and scrape away all the seeds. For a nonvegetarian appetizer, cut 1 cup of these pickles into very thin slices and toss them, along with a few tablespoons of the pickling mixture, with 1 pound of cooked, chilled shrimp. Or serve the pickles with hamburgers, hot dogs, or any dish in which you want a spicy accompaniment.

Cucumbers Pickled with Garlic and Chiles

Serves 8 to 12 as an appetizer or as a spicy flavor accent to an entrée

INGREDIENTS

2 pounds pickling cucumbers

1 tablespoon salt

1 small red bell pepper, or 3 small red chiles

12 ounces Japanese rice vinegar, unseasoned

1 cup sugar

20 paper-thin slices ginger

10 garlic cloves, peeled and crushed

2 teaspoons Asian chile sauce

ADVANCE PREPARATION

Cut each cucumber crosswise into 4 pieces. Place the cucumbers in a bowl. Add the salt and then gently toss the cucumbers until evenly coated. Set aside for 1 hour. Seed, stem, and chop the pepper or chiles. In a 2½-quart nonreactive saucepan, combine the vinegar, sugar, ginger, garlic, and chile sauce. Bring to a low boil, then cool to room temperature.

When the cucumbers have been salted for 1 hour, place the cucumbers in a colander, and rinse them with cold water to wash off the salt. Then pat the cucumbers dry. Transfer the cucumbers and the pepper or chiles to a 2-quart glass container. Pour the room-temperature vinegar mixture over the cucumbers. Make sure all the cucumbers are submerged. Place the jar in the refrigerator. The pickles will be ready to eat after 1 day and can be stored, refrigerated, for up to 1 month. Remove the pickles with a slotted spoon.

t's not surprising that Thais cook with many varieties of eggplant, since eggplant is native to Southeast Asia. In addition to the long, light purple Chinese eggplant, and the slightly shorter, dark purple Japanese type, Thai cooks use light green and yellow-streaked eggplants the size of ping-pong balls and tiny eggplants no bigger than shelled English peas. For all eggplant recipes, Asian and European, if given a choice, buy the Chinese or Japanese eggplant. Unlike the European globe eggplant, these eggplants have tender skin, fewer seeds, absorb only a little oil when sautéed, and do not taste bitter. The globe eggplant's bitter taste requires that it be salted and then rinsed and patted dry. In this recipe, eggplant is simmered in an herb-flavored coconut sauce until tender. It can then be refrigerated for hours or even overnight, then gently reheated. As a possible menu, spoon this onto your favorite pasta for a vegetarian meal, or serve as a side dish with grilled meat or seafood.

Thai Eggplant Ratatouille —————— Serves 6 to 8 as a side dish or 2 to 4 as an entrée

INGREDIENTS

10 Japanese eggplants, or 2 globe eggplants (about 1½ pounds)

½ teaspoon salt

2 yellow onions

3 tablespoons flavorless cooking oil

1½ pounds (about 5) vine-ripe tomatoes

6 cloves garlic, finely minced

2 tablespoons finely minced ginger

1 bunch chives

SAUCE

1 cup unsweetened coconut milk

¼ cup Chinese rice wine or dry sherry

2 tablespoons Thai or Vietnamese fish sauce or oyster sauce

Grated zest of 1 lime

2 teaspoons Asian chile sauce

¼ cup chopped cilantro sprigs

¼ cup chopped basil leaves

ADVANCE PREPARATION

Trim ends off eggplants. For Japanese eggplant, cut it in half lengthwise, and then cut crosswise into ½-inch-thick pieces. For globe eggplant, cut it into ½-inch-thick slices, then cut each slice into 3 by 2-inch pieces. Sprinkle the globe eggplant with the salt, and let sit 30 minutes; then rinse and pat the eggplant dry. Cut the onions into 1-inch cubes. Place a 4-quart pot over medium heat and add the cooking oil. When the oil is hot, and just gives off a wisp of smoke, add the onions. Cook the onions until they separate into layers and are deeply golden, about 10 minutes. Lower the heat if the onions begin to blacken. Cut the tomatoes in half, squeeze out the seeds, then coarsely chop the tomatoes. Combine the garlic and ginger. Chop the chives and refrigerate them.

To make the sauce, combine the coconut milk in a bowl with all the remaining ingredients.

When the onions have turned golden, add the garlic and ginger. Sauté for 30 seconds, then add the eggplant, tomatoes, and the sauce. Bring the sauce to a low boil, cover the pot, and reduce the heat to a simmer. At first the sauce will not cover all the eggplant, so remove the lid every 5 minutes, and stir the vegetables. Once all the vegetables are covered with the sauce, simmer until the eggplant becomes tender, about 20 minutes. There should be only enough sauce to just coat the vegetables. If not serving within 1 hour, then cool and refrigerate. *All advance preparation steps may be completed up to 1 day before you begin the final steps.*

FINAL STEPS

Bring the ratatouille to a simmer. Taste and adjust the seasonings, especially for salt. Transfer to heated dinner plates. Sprinkle with chives. Serve.

*T*he important step in making this complex-tasting lasagna is to first grill or broil the eggplant so that it becomes more densely textured and flavorful. Second, instead of using lasagna pasta, substitute the fresh egg-roll sheets that are sold alongside wonton wraps at supermarkets. Using these egg-roll sheets, which are a thin fresh pasta dough, results in a lighter-textured lasagna. As lasagna lovers might suspect, this is great reheated or even eaten cold. As a possible menu, accompany this dish with spinach and pine nut salad, herb garlic toast, and fresh fruit drizzled with raspberry Cabernet glaze.

Grilled Eggplant Lasagna

Serves 4 as an entrée

INGREDIENTS

6 Japanese eggplants, or 2 large eggplants (1½ pounds)

¼ cup extra virgin olive oil

Juice of 1 lemon

Salt and freshly ground black pepper

3 ears white corn

1 cup ricotta cheese

3 tablespoons hot water

4 egg-roll sheets

¼ cup grated imported Parmesan cheese

SAUCE

3 cups tomato sauce

3 tablespoons oyster sauce

1 tablespoon hoisin sauce

1 tablespoon dark sesame oil

1 tablespoon Asian chile sauce

⅓ cup chopped cilantro sprigs

4 cloves garlic, finely minced

2 tablespoons finely minced ginger

ADVANCE PREPARATION

Remove eggplant stems. If using Japanese eggplant, cut each eggplant lengthwise into 4 strips. Because the 2 outer strips would have a large amount of skin, before you begin slicing, remove the skin along both sides with the vegetable peeler, then slice the eggplant. Now the slices should have skin only along their edges. If using European eggplant, peel the eggplant. Then cut the eggplant into ¼-inch-thick slices. Sprinkle the eggplant with oil, lemon juice, salt, and pepper. Rub into the surface and marinate 15 minutes. Preheat a gas grill to medium or prepare a charcoal fire, or turn on the broiler. Brush the grill with oil. Then grill the slices until they just soften, or place them on a tray under the broiler and broil them until lightly browned on both sides, about 5 minutes of cooking.

Cut the corn kernels off the cobs. Mix the ricotta with enough hot water so that the cheese is easy to spread in a layer. Set aside the egg-roll sheets. Grate the Parmesan. In a bowl, combine all the sauce ingredients.

In an 8 by 8-inch baking pan, first place a layer of sauce that is the size of an egg-roll sheet. Add an egg-roll sheet and then begin forming the layers, adding a layer of sauce, a single layer of eggplant, a sprinkling of corn, ⅓ of the ricotta cheese, and another egg-roll sheet. Add another layer of sauce and repeat the layering, concluding with a layer of sauce, eggplant, sauce, and Parmesan cheese. *All advance preparation steps may be completed up to 8 hours before you begin the final steps.*

FINAL STEPS

Preheat the oven to 350°. Bake the lasagna for 30 minutes, uncovered, until the cheese and the sauce are bubbling. Let cool 10 minutes before slicing and serving.

ith a little advance planning, this is a beautiful salad to serve for a dinner party. The walnuts can be candied weeks in advance and stored in the freezer. Make the dressing 2 days ahead of the party. Then you will only need about 30 minutes on the day of the party to complete the simple preparation. Mango works well as a substitute for papaya, but because it does not slice into neat shapes, toss the mango slices with the endive. Avocado slices aren't a good substitution because their color is too similar to the endive. As a possible menu, accompany this dish with a hot tomato soup garnished with crème fraîche, three-grain rolls with flavored-oil dipping sauces, and strawberry shortcake.

Endive Salad with Candied Walnuts and Papaya Nests

Serves 4 as a salad course

INGREDIENTS

1½ **cups raw walnuts, shelled**
¼ **cup sugar**
¼ **teaspoon red chile flakes**
4 **ounces soft goat cheese**
2 **papayas, slightly firm**
4 **heads Belgian endive**

DRESSING

1 **small clove garlic, finely minced**
2 **tablespoons finely minced cilantro sprigs**
2 **tablespoons finely minced green onion**
1 **tablespoon finely minced ginger**
¼ **cup Japanese rice vinegar, unseasoned**
2 **tablespoons flavorless oil**
2 **tablespoons dark sesame oil**
1 **tablespoon thin soy sauce**
2 **teaspoons sugar**
½ **teaspoon Asian chile sauce**

ADVANCE PREPARATION

Preheat the oven to 350°. Bring 1 quart of water to a boil. Add the walnuts and boil for 5 minutes. Drain in a sieve. Return the saucepan to the stove and add the sugar, 2 tablespoons of water, and the chile flakes. Bring to a boil and add the walnuts. Stir the nuts until all the liquid disappears. Spread the nuts on a baking sheet lined with nonstick cooking paper, and place in the preheated oven. Roast for about 15 minutes, turning the nuts over after 7 minutes. Remove the nuts from the oven when they turn dark golden. When cool, transfer to a plastic bag, and freeze.

Crumble the goat cheese and refrigerate. Using a vegetable peeler, peel the papayas, scrape away the seeds, and cut the papayas lengthwise into ¼-inch-thick slices. Refrigerate. Separate the endive leaves. In a small bowl, combine all the ingredients for the salad dressing. *All advance preparation steps may be completed up to 8 hours before you begin the final steps.*

FINAL STEPS

On 4 salad or dinner plates, form the papaya slices into a fan shape. Place the endive leaves in a bowl. Stir the dressing, pour over the endive, and toss to combine evenly. Sprinkle on half the goat cheese, and gently toss. Place the salad next to each papaya fan. Sprinkle on the remaining goat cheese and the frozen walnuts. Serve at once.

The fennel bulbs sold in our markets are often mislabeled "sweet anise," which causes all those who dislike licorice to avoid this sweet, very delicate vegetable. Although there are many braised fennel recipes, the sublime texture and subtle flavor is quickly destroyed by cooking. On the other hand, salads are always improved by the addition of thinly sliced fennel. Interestingly, fennel seeds come from a different variety of fennel, which grows bulbless. In this recipe, fennel seeds are powdered in an electric grinder or coffee grinder and then added to the salad dressing in order to intensify the taste of the fennel. The recipe specifies imported walnut oil (most commonly from France), which has an intense flavor absent from walnut oils manufactured in the United States. You can also use another nut oil or an extra virgin olive oil. As a possible menu, accompany this dish with chilled tomato-dill soup with prawns, buttermilk biscuits, and fresh berries for dessert.

Fennel Salad with Mango-Walnut Herb Dressing

Serves 4 as a side dish

INGREDIENTS

2 heads fennel root

1 ripe mango

1 small red bell pepper

DRESSING

¼ cup freshly squeezed orange juice

2 tablespoons imported walnut oil

2 tablespoons flavorless cooking oil

2 tablespoons Japanese rice vinegar, unseasoned

½ teaspoon Asian chile sauce

½ teaspoon salt

2 tablespoons finely minced ginger

2 tablespoons chopped cilantro sprigs

1 teaspoon fennel seeds

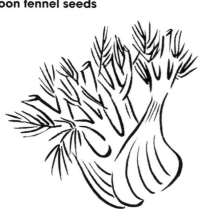

ADVANCE PREPARATION

Trim ends off the fennel root; then cut the fennel root in half. Cut each half crosswise into very thin slices, about ⅛ inch wide. Separate fennel pieces, and refrigerate. With a paring knife, peel off the mango skin, then cut the flesh off in large pieces. Cut the pieces into ¼-inch-wide strips, and refrigerate. Stem, seed, and discard the ribs from the bell pepper. Cut the pepper into ⅛-inch-wide strips, and refrigerate.

In a small bowl, combine the orange juice, oils, vinegar, chile sauce, salt, ginger, and cilantro. In an electric spice grinder or coffee grinder, powder the fennel seeds, then stir these into the dressing; refrigerate. *All advance preparation steps may be completed up to 8 hours before you begin the final steps.*

FINAL STEPS

In a bowl, combine the fennel, mango, and red pepper. Stir the dressing, and pour the dressing over the fennel. Toss all ingredients to mix well. Transfer to a platter or salad plates. Serve at once.

Greens and Leafy Salads

Until just a few years ago, only avid gardeners had the chance to make salads from baby lettuce greens. Now these tiny greens are sold by most markets even in the winter. There are many advantages to using baby greens rather than mature heads of lettuce. The leaves are more tender; there are more variations in colors, textures, and flavors; and they take only a small amount of refrigerator room. Although baby greens are sold "prewashed," for food safety and your health, always rinse them thoroughly and dry them using a lettuce spinner. A good rule is to use one handful per serving, or double that if the salad is the main entrée.

Variations for Creating Salads

Vegetables and Fruits: Choose any vegetable that can be eaten raw. Some of our favorite choices are enoki mushrooms with the root end discarded and the stems separated; raw white corn cut off the cob; ripe mango, peeled and the flesh cut into bite-sized pieces; slightly underripe papaya that is peeled (use a potato peeler), seeded, and cubed; figs cut into quarters; and perfectly ripe avocado.

Cheeses: Among many choices for salads are blue cheese, crumbled; imported and freshly grated Parmesan or Asiago; soft goat cheese, crumbled; or aged Dry Jack, grated.

Nuts: The following raw nuts are toasted in a 325° oven: pine nuts for 8 minutes; almonds, sliced or slivered, pecans, and hazelnuts for 15 minutes. After toasting the hazelnuts, rub them vigorously in a kitchen towel to remove their skins. Because walnuts are bitter tasting, boil the walnuts for 5 minutes, then roast them in a 325° oven for 30 minutes, turning the walnuts over after 15 minutes. Raw cashews taste best deep-fried. Place the cashews in a saucepan, cover the nuts with flavorless, room-temperature cooking oil, and heat the oil over high heat, stirring, until the nuts become light golden. Immediately pour the nuts into a sieve placed over another saucepan. Cool for 1 hour and pat dry with paper towels. Roasted nuts last indefinitely when frozen.

Chile Croutons: Place 2 cups bread cubes, cut from day-old French bread, into a bowl. Place ⅓ cup extra virgin olive oil, 1 tablespoon Asian chile sauce, and 3 cloves finely minced garlic in a small saucepan, and heat until the garlic sizzles in the oil but does not brown. Immediately pour the oil over the bread cubes, while stirring the cubes with a long-handled spoon.

Sprinkle the bread cubes with salt, place them on a baking sheet, and toast them in a preheated 350° oven until the croutons become golden, about 20 minutes. Remove, cool, and sprinkle with chopped cilantro. If you are not using the croutons that day, omit the cilantro, and store them in the freezer.

Chinese Wontons and Rice Sticks: Either or both of these are great gently tossed into a salad just prior to serving, or sprinkled over the top of a salad. For a salad serving 6 people, cut 14 wonton skins into ¼-inch-wide strips. Heat 2 cups flavorless cooking oil in a 10-inch sauté pan. *Caution: If the oil begins to smoke, the oil is too hot. Turn off the heat at once.* If a wonton strip, when added to the oil, bounces across the surface, the oil is hot enough. Fry the wontons in small amounts. When they become light golden, immediately transfer to a baking sheet lined with paper towels. Use the wontons the same day. For rice sticks, pull 2 ounces of rice sticks into small bundles. When the oil becomes hot enough so a rice stick expands immediately when added to the oil, fry the rice sticks a few at a time. The moment they expand (this takes about 2 to 5 seconds), turn them over and cook them on the second side for a few seconds. Immediately drain on paper towels. Crumble slightly and use the same day.

Dressings

Blue Cheese Dressing: Combine ¼ cup crumbled blue cheese, 6 tablespoons extra virgin olive oil, 3 tablespoons balsamic vinegar, 1½ tablespoons thin soy sauce, ¼ teaspoon freshly ground black pepper, and ¼ teaspoon salt.

Ginger Herb Dressing: Combine 1 teaspoon grated orange skin, ¼ cup freshly squeezed orange juice, ⅓ cup safflower oil, ¼ cup balsamic vinegar, 1 tablespoon thin soy sauce, 1 tablespoon honey, ½ teaspoon Asian chile sauce, 2 tablespoons finely minced ginger, and 2 tablespoons minced cilantro sprigs.

Creamy Lemon Garlic Dressing: Combine in an electric blender ½ cup extra virgin olive oil; ⅓ cup freshly squeezed lemon juice; 2 tablespoons mayonnaise; 1 tablespoon light brown sugar; 1 tablespoon thin soy sauce; 2 tablespoons finely minced chives, basil, or cilantro; 2 cloves garlic, finely minced; and ¼ cup freshly grated imported Parmesan cheese. Blend until smooth. Refrigerate and use that day.

F ew taste sensations are as delectable as tiny green beans picked from the garden trellis and cooked that day. Here are two of our favorite green bean recipes to use with the profusion of varieties appearing at summer farmers' markets—and in our gardens! The important thing in the recipe below is not to overcook the green beans and to combine the chilled, cooked green beans with the salad dressing just before serving. The green beans should still be crunchy and bright green. As a possible menu, accompany this dish with hot-and-sour soup and apple fritters.

Green Bean Salad with Ginger-Soy Dressing

Serves 4 to 6 as a side dish

INGREDIENTS

12 ounces any variety "green" beans

1 tablespoon toasted sesame seeds

DRESSING

¼ cup Japanese rice vinegar, unseasoned

2 tablespoons thin soy sauce

1 tablespoon dark sesame oil

1 tablespoon sugar

1 teaspoon Asian chile sauce

2 tablespoons finely minced ginger

1 whole green onion, minced

2 tablespoons chopped cilantro sprigs

ADVANCE PREPARATION

Trim the stem ends off 12 ounces of any variety of "green" beans. Bring 4 quarts of water to a rapid boil. Stir the green beans into the water. When the green beans brighten and they taste tender, about 5 minutes, immediately transfer them to a bowl containing cold water and ice. When the beans are chilled, drain and pat dry. Store in the refrigerator until ready to use. Toast the sesame seeds and set aside. In a small bowl, combine all ingredients for the salad dressing. *All advance preparation steps may be completed up to 8 hours before you begin the final steps.*

FINAL STEPS

To serve, place the green beans in a bowl, then stir the salad dressing and pour the dressing over the green beans. Stir to evenly combine. Transfer to a serving platter or salad plates. Sprinkle with 1 tablespoon toasted sesame seeds. Serve.

 n this stir-fry dish, the green beans are stir-fried and steamed until they turn bright green and become tender. After a brief stir-frying, the sauce is added and the wok covered. Every 15 to 30 seconds, remove the lid and quickly stir and toss the green beans, then cover again. The steam trapped under the lid will cook the green beans quickly. The moment the green beans taste tender and brighten in color, stir in a little cornstarch mixture to thicken the sauce. Then serve the green beans at once. As a possible menu, accompany this with barbecued shrimp, steamed jasmine rice, tomato and watercress salad, and hot peach crumble.

Stir-Fried Szechwan Green Beans————————Serves 4 as an entrée

INGREDIENTS

**12 ounces any variety
   "green" beans**

5 cloves garlic, finely minced

1 tablespoon finely minced ginger

3 tablespoons flavorless cooking oil

2 teaspoons cornstarch

SAUCE

**¼ cup Chinese rice wine or
   dry sherry**

1 tablespoon hoisin sauce

1 tablespoon oyster sauce

1 tablespoon dark sesame oil

1 tablespoon Asian chile sauce

1 tablespoon light brown sugar

1 tablespoon wine vinegar

1 whole green onion, minced

**2 tablespoons chopped
   cilantro sprigs**

ADVANCE PREPARATION

Trim the stem ends off the "green" beans. Cut the green beans, on a sharp diagonal, into 1½-inch-long pieces. In a little bowl, combine garlic, ginger, and cooking oil. Set aside cornstarch. In another bowl, combine all sauce ingredients. *All advance preparation steps may be completed up to 8 hours before you begin the final steps.*

FINAL STEPS

Combine cornstarch with an equal amount of cold water. Place a wok over highest heat. When the wok is very hot, add the garlic-oil mixture. When the garlic begins to sizzle, add the green beans. Stir and toss the green beans briefly. Add the sauce. Bring to a boil and cover the wok. Alternate cooking the green beans covered and then stir-frying the green beans until the green beans turn a bright color and taste tender. Chinese long beans and haricot verts will be cooked in about 2 minutes, while mature green beans will take about 8 minutes. As the liquid begins to evaporate, replenish it with splashes of water. When the green beans are tender, stir in a little of the cornstarch mixture to lightly thicken the sauce. Transfer to a heated platter or dinner plates. Serve at once.

BOK CHOY

CHINESE BROCCOLI

CHINESE CELERY

NAPA CABBAGE

CHINESE CHIVES

JAPANESE CUCUMBER

Hot New Asian Vegetables

The variety of vegetables in Asia is so staggering that it makes the selection of vegetables in our markets seem limited, if not dreary. Luckily, many American supermarkets have felt Asia's influence. Here is a brief description and cooking information about Asian vegetables. If some of these are not yet in your corner supermarket, they will be within a few years.

Long Beans (pictured on page 57): Available in both dark and light green varieties, these beans, which stretch nearly 2 feet in length, cook very quickly. Cut them into 2-inch pieces and stir-fry, sauté, or blanch and add to salads.

Bok Choy (Chinese White Cabbage): There are over twenty different varieties of this cabbage, ranging from mature bok choy to little baby plants. The leaves and stems take the same amount of time to cook. Cut the stems on a diagonal and each leaf, if large, into 4 pieces. Best stir-fried.

Chinese Broccoli (Chinese Kale, Gai Lan): This has a more intense flavor than American broccoli. Both the stems and the leaves are eaten. Cook it exactly the same way as you would American broccoli. It is great sautéed, stir-fried, or blanched and added to salads.

Napa Cabbage (Celery Cabbage, Chinese Cabbage): The most important leafy vegetable in northern China, napa cabbage is best stir-fried, though it is delicious sautéed in butter with garlic, chopped tomatoes, and basil.

Chinese Celery (Smallage, Hon Kun): This has a more intense flavor than American celery. In Asian cooking, celery is not eaten raw, but rather stir-fried, added to soup, or braised. It is also very good blanched in boiling water and chilled in ice water before being tossed with a salad dressing.

Chinese Chives (Gow Choy): Chinese chives come in three varieties: green, yellow, and garlic chives. They are all stronger flavored than European chives, but can be used the same way.

Japanese Cucumber: These small, very crisp cucumbers have no bitter taste and are great pickled or eaten raw in salads.

Asian Eggplant (Chinese or Japanese Eggplant): These are superior in taste and texture to the large globe eggplant. Do not peel. They are great stir-fried, sautéed, and grilled. All European eggplant recipes will be improved by substituting these Asian eggplants.

Lotus Root (Water Lily): This segmented root has a very attractive tunnel system. Using a potato peeler, remove the skin, then cut crosswise into paper-thin slices and pickle.

Chinese Okra (Angled Luffa): Chinese okra has a flavor and texture similar to zucchini. To prepare it, pare off the ridges and scrape the skin lightly. Cut it crosswise or into cubes, and stir-fry it, or add to soups or stews.

Asian Radish (Daikon, Japanese radish): These giant, mild-tasting white radishes called "daikon" are now commonly available. Peel and cut the flesh into matchstick-shaped pieces for salads, or into larger pieces to serve as an appetizer with dips. Japanese radish is also excellent pickled.

Water Chestnuts (Ma Tai): Utterly different tasting than the canned type, fresh water chestnuts, which grow in flooded fields, taste like very crisp apples crossed with sweet, juicy coconuts. When buying, squeeze each water chestnut and discard any that feel soft since these will be rotten in the center. Water chestnuts are very muddy, so using a small paring knife, peel them under slowly running cold water. Unpeeled water chestnuts will last for up to 10 days refrigerated. To store once peeled, they do not need to be submerged in water. Place peeled water chestnuts in a plastic storage bag and refrigerate. Use within 1 day. Slice and eat fresh water chestnuts raw in salads, stir-fry them, or add them to soups and to stews. They will still be crisp no matter how long they cook.

Winter Melon (Winter Gourd): Winter melon is a giant member of the squash family with a very mild taste. Cut the white flesh into large pieces and simmer it in soups until translucent.

Hairy Melon (not pictured): A member of the squash family, the hairy melon has an outer fuzz that must be scrubbed away. Then use the melon exactly the way you would zucchini.

ASIAN EGGPLANT

LOTUS ROOT

CHINESE OKRA

ASIAN RADISH

WATER CHESTNUTS

WINTER MELON

J icama, the brown-skinned and round tuber sold by most supermarkets, is pronounced "HEE-kah-mah." It's part of the morning glory family and ranges in size from a grapefruit to a small melon. Beneath the brown skin lies the white, very crisp, and slightly sweet flesh. Although some cookbooks recommend peeling jicama, we find that the only efficient way to remove the skin and its underlying thin fibrous surface is to cut the skin off with a knife. Prepared in matchstick-sized pieces, it's great in salads, or as an appetizer accompanied by a dip. Jicama will not discolor if cut 12 hours in advance, sealed in a plastic bag, and refrigerated. The unused part of the root will last for about 2 weeks if wrapped tightly with plastic wrap and refrigerated. In this salad, we love the flavor imparted by using the imported French virgin pecan oil, but extra virgin olive oil or walnut oil works fine too. As a possible menu, accompany this dish with roasted vegetable stew, corn bread muffins flecked with herbs, and homemade peach ice cream.

Jicama Tex-Mex Salad
Serves 4 as a salad

INGREDIENTS

1 cup pecan halves

1 pound jicama

1 large bunch watercress

1 red bell pepper

DRESSING

¼ cup freshly squeezed lime juice

3 tablespoons French virgin pecan oil

3 tablespoons honey

½ teaspoon Asian chile sauce

½ teaspoon ground cumin

½ teaspoon salt

1 small clove garlic, finely minced

2 tablespoons chopped cilantro sprigs

ADVANCE PREPARATION

Preheat the oven to 325°, then roast the pecans for 15 minutes. Using a knife, trim off the jicama skin. Cut the jicama into ¼-inch-wide slices. Stack the slices and cut them into matchstick-shaped pieces. You will need a total of 4 cups. Place the pieces in a plastic bag and refrigerate. Wash the watercress, discard any tough ends, and refrigerate. Char the red bell pepper over a gas flame or under an electric broiler coil. When the bell pepper is lightly charred on all sides, transfer it to a paper or plastic bag and close the bag. After 10 minutes, rub away any blackened skin, then stem, seed, and cut the pepper into matchstick pieces; refrigerate. In a small bowl, combine the lime juice with all the remaining ingredients. Refrigerate. *All advance preparation steps may be completed up to 8 hours before you begin the final steps.*

FINAL STEPS

In a large bowl, combine the jicama, watercress, red pepper, and nuts. Stir the dressing and pour over the jicama. Toss all the ingredients until they are evenly coated with the salad dressing. Transfer the salad to a salad platter or salad plates, and serve.

 **A**lthough this mushroom sauce takes about 1 hour to prepare, all the steps are easy. It's not only delicious spooned on top of or mixed into any type of pasta, it's also great placed underneath steaks, chicken, or fish that has been cooked on the grill. Or, add an equal amount of vegetable broth and heavy cream to create a savory soup. As a possible menu, accompany this dish with Asian greens, bread, and sautéed bananas with Grand Marnier.

Mushrooms with Pasta, Red Wine, and Thyme

Serves 4 as an entrée

INGREDIENTS

8 ounces dried penne, fusilli, or your favorite pasta

½ cup chopped parsley

2 ounces imported Parmesan cheese

1 tablespoon cornstarch

SAUCE

2 small yellow onions, chopped

4 cloves garlic, minced

1½ pounds mushrooms (shiitake, portobello, chanterelle, cremini, or hedgehog)

1 cup red wine, such as zinfandel

1 cup vegetable or chicken broth

2 tablespoons oyster sauce

1 tablespoon heavy soy sauce

2 teaspoons tomato paste

½ teaspoon Asian chile sauce

½ teaspoon sugar

1 tablespoon chopped fresh thyme leaves

6 tablespoons unsalted butter

Salt and freshly ground black pepper to taste

ADVANCE PREPARATION

Set aside the pasta, parsley, cheese, and cornstarch in separate containers. Place the onions and garlic in seperate containers. Discard the stems from the shiitake and portobello mushrooms. Cut the mushrooms into ¼-inch-wide pieces. In a small bowl, combine the wine, broth, oyster sauce, soy sauce, tomato paste, chile sauce, sugar, and thyme.

Place a 12-inch sauté pan that is not cast iron or aluminum over medium heat. Add half the butter, and when the butter is melted, add the onions. Sauté the onions until they become golden, about 15 minutes. Then add the remaining butter, the garlic, and the mushrooms. Cook the mushrooms until they soften, expel all their moisture and eventually become densely textured, about 10 to 15 minutes. Add wine sauce, bring to a boil over medium heat, and cook until mushrooms begin to show above the sauce, about 6 minutes. Cool, transfer to a bowl, and refrigerate the sauce. *All advance preparation steps may be completed up to 8 hours before you begin the final steps.*

FINAL STEPS

Grate the cheese. Combine the cornstarch with an equal amount of cold water. Bring 4 quarts of water to a rapid boil. Lightly salt the water then cook the pasta according to the instructions on the package. When the pasta loses its raw texture but is still slightly firm, tip the pasta and the water into a colander. Return the pasta pot to the stove over high heat. Add the mushroom sauce and bring to a low boil. Stir in a little of the cornstarch mixture to slightly thicken the sauce. Return the pasta to the pot, and stir to evenly combine. Add salt and pepper to taste. Transfer the pasta to a heated serving platter or dinner plates. Sprinkle on the parsley and grated cheese. Serve at once.

This tart makes perfect winter fare. It can be prepared in the morning, and then the only remaining steps are the baking and eating. One word of caution: caramelize the onions slowly. Attempting to quicken the process just burns the onions. If in doubt, lower the heat. As a possible menu, accompany this dish with a baby green salad or a soup, warm baguettes, imported olives, and chocolate truffles and fresh fruit.

Onion Caramelized Tart

Serves 4 as an entrée

INGREDIENTS

1 cup unbleached white flour

½ teaspoon salt

8 tablespoons chilled unsalted butter, cut in small pieces

3 tablespoons ice water

1 egg, beaten

FILLING

8 cups thinly sliced yellow onion, about 5 onions

¼ cup unsalted butter

5 cloves garlic, minced

½ pound button mushrooms, thinly sliced

2 tablespoons unbleached white flour

½ cup heavy cream, warmed

1 cup grated imported Parmesan cheese

¼ cup chopped parsley

2 tablespoons fresh oregano leaves, chopped

½ teaspoon salt

½ teaspoon freshly ground black pepper

¼ chopped chives

ADVANCE PREPARATION

To make the tart dough, place the flour, salt, and butter in a food processor. Process until the flour mixture resembles cornmeal. With the machine on, add ice water and process until the dough just begins to stick together. Remove the dough from the processor and press together into a ball. Roll out the dough on a floured surface into a thin sheet; then transfer the dough to a 10-inch tart pan. Press into the sides of the pan. Brush with beaten egg.

To make the filling, slice the onions. In a large sauté pan, melt the ¼ cup of butter. Add the onions and cook over medium heat until they turn golden, about 15 minutes. Meanwhile, have the remaining ingredients ready. When the onions are golden, add the garlic and mushrooms. Sauté until the mushrooms shrink drastically in size, about 5 minutes.

Sprinkle on the flour and sauté for 2 minutes. Add the cream, Parmesan, parsley, oregano, salt, and pepper. Cook until it becomes very thick. Allow the filling to cool completely and then spread it evenly over the pastry shell. Sprinkle on the chives. If assembled more than 1 hour prior to baking, then refrigerate. *All advance preparation steps may be completed up to 8 hours before you begin the final steps.*

FINAL STEPS

Preheat oven to 375°. Place the tart in the oven and bake until it is golden on top, about 40 minutes. Let the tart sit at room temperature for 10 minutes before cutting it into wedges. Serve.

on't be intimidated by the long list of ingredients. This onion stew is easy to make. Everything can be prepared in the morning, and then, that evening, before the dinner guests arrive, the biscuit dough can be rolled out and fitted over the onion stew. Cooked in the oven until the stew is piping hot, the biscuit crust rises, turns a beautiful gold, and substitutes for the ubiquitous dinner rolls. I always make an extra amount of the biscuit dough, and then form little rolls. Placed on the baking sheet that holds the onion stew, these "extra" biscuits never go uneaten. As a possible menu, accompany this dish with Caesar salad with fresh corn and roasted red pepper, and chocolate crème brûlée.

Onions Stewed with a Biscuit Crust

Serves 4 to 6 as a side dish or 4 as an entrée

INGREDIENTS

4 to 6 yellow onions
4 medium carrots, peeled
½ pound cremini mushrooms
4 tablespoons unsalted butter
2 tablespoons white flour
6 cloves garlic, minced
½ cup heavy cream
⅓ cup dry vermouth or white wine
¼ cup vegetable or chicken broth
½ teaspoon Asian chile sauce
½ teaspoon grated orange zest
½ teaspoon salt
¼ cup chopped tarragon leaves
¼ cup chopped parsley

BISCUIT CRUST

1 cup unbleached white flour
1 teaspoon baking powder
½ teaspoon salt
¼ teaspoon baking soda
4 tablespoons unsalted butter, cut into small pieces
½ cup buttermilk

ADVANCE PREPARATION

To make the stew, peel the onions; cut each onion in half, and then in ½-inch-wide slices so that you have 8 cups of sliced onions. Cut the carrots into ¼-inch-wide slices, on a sharp diagonal. Cut the mushrooms into ¼-inch-wide slices. Have ready the butter, flour, and garlic. In a small bowl, combine the cream, vermouth, broth, chile sauce, orange zest, salt, tarragon, and parsley.

Place a 12-inch skillet over medium heat and add the butter. When the butter is melted, add the onions. Cook them until they brown lightly, about 15 minutes. Then add the garlic, carrots, and mushrooms. Sauté until the mushrooms shrink in size, about 5 minutes. Stir the flour into the onions. Add the sauce. Bring the sauce to a low boil and cook until it becomes very thick. Taste and adjust the seasonings. Transfer the onion stew to a 12-inch oval ovenproof baking dish. Cool and refrigerate.

To make the crust, place the flour, baking powder, salt, baking soda, and butter in a food processor. Turn the machine on and process for 30 seconds. With the machine still on, slowly pour the buttermilk down the feed tube. Stop the moment the mixture begins to form into lumps. Lightly flour your hands, press the dough together, and wrap it in plastic wrap. Keep at room temperature. *All advance preparation steps may be completed up to 8 hours before you begin the final steps.*

FINAL STEPS

Within 1 hour of cooking, roll the biscuit dough into a sheet large enough to cover the stew. Fit it over the stew, seal around the sides, then pierce the dough to make little steam vents. Preheat the oven to 375°. Place the stew in the preheated oven. Cook until the stew is thoroughly reheated and the crust becomes brown, about 20 minutes. Serve at once.

Parsnips, which Europeans brought to America in the seventeenth century, have never achieved much popularity here. Yet there are few vegetables as satisfying to eat as parsnips rubbed with extra virgin olive oil, garlic, and salt, and then barbecued, or parsnips peeled, boiled in water, and mashed in the manner used for mashing potatoes. In this recipe, parsnips are cut into bite-sized pieces and sautéed in a ginger-citrus sauce that has a hint of chile, cinnamon, and herbs. As a possible menu, accompany this dish with a barbecued, butterflied leg of lamb, hot flour tortillas, baby greens tossed with extra virgin olive oil and salt, and Key lime ice cream.

Parsnips in Gingered Orange Sauce

Serves 4 to 6 as a side dish

INGREDIENTS

6 medium parsnips, about 1½ pounds

¼ cup unsalted butter

1 teaspoon grated orange zest

2 cups freshly squeezed orange juice

¼ cup Japanese rice vinegar, unseasoned

¼ cup light brown sugar

2 tablespoons thin soy sauce

2 tablespoons finely minced ginger

1 teaspoon ground cinnamon

1 teaspoon Asian chile sauce

1 tablespoon cornstarch

¼ cup cilantro sprigs or basil leaves

ADVANCE PREPARATION

Peel the parsnips. Cut them in half lengthwise; then cut each half on a sharp diagonal in ¼-inch-thick pieces. You will have about 4 to 5 cups. Refrigerate the parsnips. Set aside the butter. Combine the grated orange zest, half the orange juice, the vinegar, sugar, soy sauce, ginger, cinnamon, and chile sauce; refrigerate. Refrigerate the remaining orange juice. Set aside the cornstarch. Keep the herbs refrigerated. *All advance preparation steps may be completed up to 8 hours before you begin the final steps.*

FINAL STEPS

Combine the cornstarch with an equal amount of cold water. Chop the herbs. Place a 12-inch sauté pan over medium heat. Add the butter, and when it melts, add the parsnips. Stir and toss until they begin to brown, then add the sauce. Bring the sauce to a low boil, cover, and steam-cook on medium. Cook the parsnips until they are tender when pierced with a fork, about 8 minutes. If the sauce appears about to boil away, add a splash of the reserved orange juice. When the parsnips are tender, if nearly all the liquid has boiled away, add ½ cup of orange juice. When it comes to a boil, stir in just enough of the cornstarch mixture so the sauce lightly glazes the parsnips. Stir in the herbs. Taste and adjust the seasonings. Transfer to dinner plates. Serve at once.

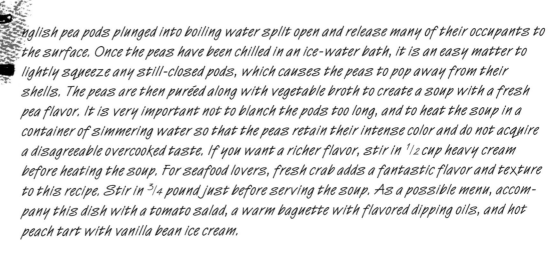

English pea pods plunged into boiling water split open and release many of their occupants to the surface. Once the peas have been chilled in an ice-water bath, it is an easy matter to lightly squeeze any still-closed pods, which causes the peas to pop away from their shells. The peas are then puréed along with vegetable broth to create a soup with a fresh pea flavor. It is very important not to blanch the pods too long, and to heat the soup in a container of simmering water so that the peas retain their intense color and do not acquire a disagreeable overcooked taste. If you want a richer flavor, stir in $^1/_2$ cup heavy cream before heating the soup. For seafood lovers, fresh crab adds a fantastic flavor and texture to this recipe. Stir in $^3/_4$ pound just before serving the soup. As a possible menu, accompany this dish with a tomato salad, a warm baguette with flavored dipping oils, and hot peach tart with vanilla bean ice cream.

Pea Soup with Garlic and Cheese Croutons

Serves 6 to 8 as a first course or 4 as an entrée

INGREDIENTS

2 tablespoons minced ginger

1 shallot, peeled and chopped

$^1/_4$ cup unsalted butter

2 pounds fresh English peas, unshelled

2 cups vegetable broth

$^1/_2$ cup heavy cream, optional

1 teaspoon salt

$^1/_4$ teaspoon finely ground white pepper

CROUTONS

6-inch length of baguette

2 tablespoons extra virgin olive oil

2 cloves garlic, finely minced

1 cup grated Gruyère cheese

ADVANCE PREPARATION

Prepare the ginger and shallot. Place a 2-quart saucepan over medium heat. Add the ginger, shallot, and butter. When the butter melts and the shallot begins to sizzle but has not browned, set the saucepan aside.

Fill an 8-quart stockpot half full of water, place over high heat and bring the water to a vigorous boil. Fill a large bowl with ice and cold water. Add the pea pods to the boiling water. Stir the pods until they turn a bright green and some of the peas are released from the pods, about 2 minutes. Immediately tip the peas and pods into a colander and transfer the peas and pods to the ice water. When chilled, using your fingers, gently press any pods that have not opened in order to release their peas. Discard all the pods, and set aside the peas. You should have about 2$^1/_4$ cups of peas.

Place the peas in an electric blender. Add the vegetable broth and liquefy. Strain through a medium-meshed sieve into the saucepan holding the butter, ginger, and shallot. Refrigerate.

To make the croutons, preheat the oven to 400°. Cut the bread, on a sharp diagonal, into $^1/_4$-inch-wide slices. Brush one side of the slices with oil. Place the bread, oiled side up, on a baking sheet, and toast the slices in the oven until crisp but not browned. Set aside. Mince the garlic and grate the cheese. *All advance preparation steps may be completed up to 8 hours before you begin the final steps.*

FINAL STEPS

Place the bread slices, oiled side up, on a baking sheet. Sprinkle the bread with garlic and cheese. Turn the oven to broil. Place the saucepan holding the soup inside a larger saucepan holding simmering water. If you use heavy cream, stir this in now. Bring the soup to a simmer. Taste and adjust the seasonings, adding salt and white pepper. Ladle the soup into heated soup bowls. Place the bread under the broiler until the cheese melts. Place one slice in each bowl. Serve at once.

ome-roasted peppers have a many-faceted taste and firm texture quite different from the roasted peppers sold in small glass jars by supermarkets. It takes only minutes to sear peppers over a gas flame or under an electric broiler, and then it is a simple matter to rub off the charred skin. Roast peppers when you want more flavor and a less watery texture. Roasted peppers are great in salads, as a garnish in cream-based soups, in sandwiches, chopped and placed in dumpling fillings, and in pizzas. In this recipe, you could substitute your favorite pizza dough for ours, or even buy pizza dough from an Italian restaurant. But there's no replacement for the pizza paddle for efficiently transferring the pizza in and out of the oven, and a pizza stone is essential for crisping the underside of the pizza crust. As a possible menu, accompany this dish with a spinach-walnut salad and raspberry cobbler for dessert.

Pizza with Roasted Pepper Topping

Serves 6 to 10 as an appetizer and 2 to 4 as an entrée

INGREDIENTS

2 cups unbleached white flour

3 tablespoons semolina flour (optional)

3 tablespoons chopped cilantro sprigs or basil leaves

¾ cup warm water

2 teaspoons dry yeast

1 tablespoon sugar

1 tablespoon extra virgin olive oil

1½ teaspoons salt

¼ cup cornmeal

TOPPING

2 tablespoons extra virgin olive oil

3 garlic cloves, finely minced

½ teaspoon dried red chile flakes

3 to 4 bell peppers, various colors

3 ounces aged Gouda, imported Parmesan, or goat cheese

¼ cup chopped basil leaves or cilantro sprigs

ADVANCE PREPARATION

To make the pizza dough, combine the flours and chopped herbs. In another bowl, combine the water, yeast, and sugar. When the yeast bubbles, add the olive oil and salt. Add the water mixture to the flour. Stir, then turn the dough onto a floured surface and knead it until it is soft and no longer sticky, about 5 minutes. Transfer it to a bowl that has been lightly coated with olive oil; rotate the dough so that it is lightly coated in oil, cover, and let the dough rise until it doubles in size, about 1 to 2 hours. Then punch down. If making the dough more than 3 hours ahead, let the dough rise in the refrigerator.

To make the topping, combine the olive oil, garlic, and chile. Roast the peppers over a gas flame turned to the highest setting, and cook the peppers until they are blackened on all sides, or blacken them under an electric broiler. Transfer the peppers to a paper or plastic bag, twist the bag shut, and set aside for 5 minutes. Then rub off the charred skin; stem, seed, and cut the peppers into matchstick- or triangle-shaped pieces. Shred the Gouda or Parmesan, or crumble the goat cheese and refrigerate. *All advance preparation steps may be completed up to 8 hours before you begin the final steps.*

FINAL STEPS

Place a large pizza stone in the oven and preheat the oven to 500° for 1 hour. Chop the herbs. Using a rolling pin, roll the pizza dough until it is slightly larger than the pizza paddle. Rub the surface of the dough with the olive oil, garlic, and chile flakes. Sprinkle a pizza paddle or baking sheet with cornmeal. Gently lay the pizza dough on top of the paddle. Fold the edges of the dough inward to create an irregular crust. Sprinkle on the peppers and cheese. Slide the pizza onto the pizza stone. Bake the pizza until the crust becomes golden, about 12 minutes. Remove the pizza from the oven, sprinkle it with herbs, cut it into wedges, and serve at once.

ach summer we look forward to seeing what new odd-colored or shaped peppers will appear at the local farmers' market. Next to one display of peppers is the "pepper man," who chars peppers by turning a perforated drum filled with fresh peppers that are gradually blackened over a hot propane flame. His peppers, picked early that morning, whether roasted, eaten raw, or as in the following recipe, given a quick stir-frying, have a texture and intensity of flavor very different from supermarket peppers. We have enjoyed this recipe as a vegetarian main entrée served with steamed jasmine rice, and also as a side dish to accompany grilled fish. The combination of Grand Marnier and curry adds a wonderful exotic flavor. As a possible menu, accompany this dish with fennel salad, basmati rice scented with saffron, and chocolate ice cream with mango sauce.

Peppers with Caribbean Curry and Grand Marnier

Serves 4 to 6 as a side dish or 2 to 3 as an entrée

INGREDIENTS

5 to 6 bell peppers, various colors

1 small yellow onion

½ cup dried raisins or currants

½ cup slivered almonds

3 tablespoons flavorless cooking oil

4 cloves garlic, finely minced

2 tablespoons finely minced ginger

2 fresh serrano chiles, minced

2 teaspoons curry powder

SAUCE

1 vine-ripe tomato, seeded and
    chopped

½ cup vegetable or chicken broth

2 tablespoons thin soy sauce

2 tablespoons Grand Marnier

1 tablespoon oyster sauce

1 tablespoon light brown sugar

Zest of 1 lime, minced

Juice of 1 lime

2 teaspoons cornstarch

ADVANCE PREPARATION

Preheat the oven to 325°. Seed and stem the peppers. Cut the peppers into rectangular pieces, about ½ by 1 inch. Peel and chop the onion. You should have about 4 to 5 cups of vegetables. Combine all the vegetables and the raisins. Toast the almonds in the preheated oven until golden, about 15 minutes. Combine the cooking oil, garlic, ginger, chiles, and curry powder.

To make the sauce, in a small bowl, combine the tomato with all the remaining ingredients and then refrigerate. *All advance preparation steps may be completed up to 8 hours before you begin the final steps.*

FINAL STEPS

Place a 14- to 16-inch wok or a large sauté pan over highest heat. When the pan becomes very hot, add the oil-garlic mixture. Sauté for a few seconds, and then add the vegetables. Stir and toss until the peppers become brightly colored, about 3 minutes. Stir the sauce and then add it to the vegetables. Stir and toss until the vegetables are well coated with the sauce, about 30 seconds. Stir in the nuts. Immediately transfer to a heated serving platter or dinner plates. Serve at once.

ccording to potato authorities, medium-starch potatoes such as long whites, Yukon gold, or Finnish yellow are best for gratins, mashing, and roasting. Higher-starch potatoes such as russets, also called "baking" or "Idaho" potatoes, are better for roasting, mashing, or for making french fries. Although the low-starch little red potatoes are supposed to be best boiled and used in salads, we often rub these with garlic, extra virgin olive oil, salt, and pepper, and roast them in a 425° oven. Fantastic! While all the preparation steps for this gratin are easy, the gratin does require about 1 hour of preparation time in order to roast the garlic, caramelize the onions, and to carefully layer the potato slices. As a possible menu, accompany this dish with garden tomato salad and lemon cake with a berry topping.

Potato Gratin with Roasted Garlic

Serves 4 as a side dish or 2 as an entrée

INGREDIENTS

1 head garlic

1 tablespoon extra virgin olive oil

¼ cup unsalted butter

1 large yellow onion

2 pounds Yukon gold or other medium-starch potato

1½ cups heavy cream, half-and-half, or milk

2 teaspoons freshly ground nutmeg

1 teaspoon salt

1 teaspoon Asian chile sauce

2 tablespoons minced fresh rosemary

¼ cup chopped parsley or chives

1 cup grated Gruyère cheese

ADVANCE PREPARATION

Preheat the oven to 400°. Cut off the top quarter of the garlic head and drizzle oil over the exposed garlic; wrap the garlic in aluminum foil, and roast in the preheated oven for 1 hour. Then remove the head of garlic, and when it is cool, squeeze out all the garlic cloves and reserve.

Using half the butter, butter an 8 by 8-inch Pyrex baking dish. Peel and thinly slice the onion. Place a 10-inch sauté pan over medium heat and add the remaining butter. When the butter bubbles, add the onion. Over low heat, cook the onion until dark golden, about 15 minutes, then set it aside.

Peel the potatoes, then cut them crosswise in ⅛-inch-thick slices; submerge the slices in cold water. In a bowl, combine 1 cup cream, nutmeg, salt, chile sauce, and rosemary. Place all the roasted, peeled garlic cloves in a food processor. Mince briefly. Then add the cream mixture, and process 10 more seconds. Refrigerate the chopped parsley.

Dry the potato slices with paper towels. Cut half the slices in half. Fit one layer of potatoes tightly across the surface of the Pyrex baking dish, using the potato halves along the sides, in the corners, and to fill any gaps. Add the onion in an even layer, and then half the cheese and ⅓ of the cream mixture. Add another layer of potato, the cheese, and cream. Add the final potato layer, topping it with the remaining cheese and cream. Shake the pan and gently press the potatoes. If the cream mixture does not rise to the top layer of potatoes, add extra cream. Refrigerate. *All advance preparation steps may be completed up to 8 hours before you begin the final steps.*

FINAL STEPS

Preheat the oven to 325°. Place the baking dish in the preheated oven, and bake until the potatoes are tender and golden on top, about 1 hour. If you turn the oven down to 200°, the potatoes can be kept warm for 1 hour. To serve, sprinkle with parsley or chives.

There are many ways to vary mashed potatoes, such as adding roasted garlic cloves; freshly chopped herbs, including chives, parsley, or cilantro; or adding the very peppery horseradish root, which has a flavor not duplicated with the bottled horseradish varieties. Sold by many markets, horseradish is a light brown, 6- to 10-inch root, somewhat resembling the size and color of a small parsnip. In terms of technique, mash the potatoes with a potato masher or the tongs of a large fork, or force the potatoes through a food mill. But never beat the potatoes in an electric mixer or food processor, because that quickly develops the gluten and results in a leaden texture. As a possible menu, accompany this dish with beef tenderloin or barbecued summer vegetables, asparagus and baby greens salad, and apple tart.

Mashed Potatoes with Garlic and Horseradish Root
Serves 8 as a side dish

INGREDIENTS
4 pounds russet or Yukon gold potatoes

4 cloves garlic

2-inch piece horseradish root, or ½ cup bottled horseradish

1 cup heavy cream or half-and-half

½ cup butter

Salt to taste

¼ cup chopped chives

½ cup freshly grated imported Parmesan cheese

FOOD MILL

ADVANCE PREPARATION
Place 6 quarts cold water in a large pot. Peel the potatoes; then cut them in half and submerge them in the water. Peel the garlic. Using a vegetable peeler, remove and discard the horseradish root skin, then thinly slice enough of the root to fill ¼ cup. Place the garlic, sliced horseradish, ¼ cup of the cream, and ¼ cup water in an electric blender; liquefy. If the mixture is very thick, then add a little more water. Place the horse-radish liquid and the remaining cream in a small saucepan and refrigerate. Cut the butter into 8 pieces. Place the pieces on a plate and refrigerate. Set aside, separately, the salt, chives, and cheese. *All advance preparation steps may be completed up to 8 hours before you begin the final steps.*

FINAL STEPS
Bring the butter to room temperature. Bring the water to a boil. Cook the potatoes at a low boil until the potatoes become tender, about 20 minutes once the water comes to a boil. Once the potatoes become tender, drain the potatoes into a colander. If serving the potatoes right away, return the potatoes to the pot in which they were boiled. Heat the horseradish cream to a simmer. Mash the potatoes with a potato masher or the tongs of a large fork, mashing in the butter and the heated cream. When no lumps remain, stir in salt to taste, chives, and cheese. Spoon the potatoes onto heated dinner plates, or transfer the potatoes to a pastry bag, pipe the potatoes onto a baking sheet, and brown the edges by placing the potatoes under the broiler. Serve at once.

If planning not to serve the mashed potatoes right away: Once the potatoes are mashed and seasoned as described above, transfer the potatoes to a small saucepan and place this inside a larger saucepan holding simmering water. Cover the mashed potatoes with plastic wrap. *All advance preparation and cooking steps may be completed up to 2 hours before you serve the mashed potatoes.* Spoon the potatoes onto heated dinner plates. Serve at once.

*A*lthough this dish takes about 1 hour to prepare, the preparation steps are extremely simple. Yet this soup will have guests thinking that you worked for days. We have enjoyed creating many variations, such as stirring 1 pound of fresh crabmeat into the soup just before serving or decorating the soup with dots of ancho-chile jam from page 43 or, when pumpkin is not available, substituting any variety of winter squash. As a possible menu, accompany this dish with a chilled shrimp appetizer, a green salad, hot sourdough rolls, and a strawberry tart.

Pumpkin Soup with Cilantro Swirl

Serves 10 as a first course or 6 as an entrée

INGREDIENTS

1 (5-pound) pumpkin, or 5 cups canned pumpkin purée

2 tablespoons finely minced ginger

6 cups vegetable or chicken broth

1 cup heavy cream

2 teaspoons freshly grated nutmeg

1 teaspoon salt

½ teaspoon finely ground white pepper

1 cup crème fraîche or plain yogurt

1 cup cilantro sprigs, packed

2 tablespoons freshly squeezed lemon juice

ADVANCE PREPARATION

Preheat the oven to 400°. Cut the pumpkin into 4 pieces. Scrape out and discard the seeds. Place the pumpkin in the preheated oven and bake for 1 hour. Then remove the pumpkin and scrape out the softened flesh. Purée the flesh in a food processor or electric blender, adding the ginger and enough vegetable broth and cream to liquefy. You should end up with 12 cups of liquid. Add nutmeg, salt, and pepper. Stir well and refrigerate.

Set aside half of the crème fraîche. Place the remaining crème fraîche, cilantro, and lemon juice in an electric blender and liquefy. Then refrigerate. *All advance preparation steps may be completed up to 8 hours before you begin the final steps.*

FINAL STEPS

In a saucepan, bring the soup to a simmer; taste and adjust the seasonings, especially the salt. Ladle the soup into heated soup bowls. Decorate the top of the soup with dots or swirls of cilantro purée and crème fraîche. Serve at once.

R*adicchio, unknown in this country a decade ago, has found enough favor with our cooks so that it's now sold by supermarkets year-round. Most closely associated with Italy's Veneto region, these heads of chicory, about the size of Bibb lettuce, can range from the common red bundles to some varieties having variegated or speckled leaves. The slightly bitter leaves are a marvelous addition in many salads, but remove the white stem area, which is tough. Always buy radicchio with firm heads and without brown spots. Although we have seen recipes for grilling, broiling, and sautéing radicchio, we don't recommend these techniques because the radicchio quickly becomes a shriveled, brown mess. In this salad, the bitterness and crunch of radicchio contrast nicely with the sweet and somewhat soft textures of the fruits. As a possible menu, accompany this dish with an entrée of chilled salmon, bulgur wheat salad, and fudge cake.*

Radicchio Salad with Bananas and Avocados

Serves 6 as a first course or 4 as an entrée

INGREDIENTS

2 medium heads radicchio
4 to 6 dates, or 8 figs
2 firm bananas
2 ripe avocados

DRESSING

3 tablespoons safflower oil
2 tablespoons lime juice, freshly squeezed
2 tablespoons Thai or Vietnamese fish sauce
2 tablespoons light brown sugar
2 teaspoons Asian chile sauce
1 tablespoon finely minced ginger
1 tablespoon chopped mint leaves
1 tablespoon chopped cilantro sprigs

ADVANCE PREPARATION

Pull apart the radicchio leaves, then tear away and discard the bitter white stem area; you should have about 4 cups. Refrigerate the radicchio. Pit the dates and thinly slice, or thinly slice the figs and refrigerate. Set aside the bananas and avocados. In a small bowl, combine the dressing and refrigerate. *All advance preparation steps may be completed up to 8 hours before you begin the final steps.*

FINAL STEPS

Slice the bananas. Cut the avocados in half, remove the pit, scoop out the flesh, and cut into ¼-inch slices. Stir the dressing. Place the radicchio in a bowl and toss with just enough of the dressing to barely coat the leaves. Transfer the leaves to salad plates. Place the dates or figs, banana slices, and avocado slices in the bowl, add the dressing, and then gently toss the dates, bananas, and avocados with the dressing. Place on top of the radicchio. Serve at once.

BEETS

Root Vegetables
Often-Overlooked Treasures

KOHLRABI

I t's worthwhile to investigate the use of some of the following root vegetables. They are a good, inexpensive source of vitamins and minerals, they store well, and they are widely available throughout the year.

Beets: Beet cooking has been revolutionized by the many "new" varieties of baby beets now sold at farmers' markets. Baby beets are great roasted, then peeled and sliced, and added to salads. Or just scrub baby beets and place them directly into stews to simmer until they become tender, about 30 minutes. Mature beets are great roasted in a 400° oven until tender, about 1 hour. Cut away the skin and eat the beets seasoned with salt, pepper, lemon juice, and butter or olive oil.

Kohlrabies: Kohlrabi, whose name means "cabbage turnip" in German, is a swollen stem that grows aboveground. It is a member of the turnip family. Young kohlrabi is wonderful shredded or cut into matchstick-shaped pieces and used raw in salads or as an appetizer with dips. More mature kohlrabi is best roasted or simmered in stews. The young leaves are excellent stir-fried.

Parsnips: Parsnips have an alluring nutty sweetness. They are great peeled, cut into 2-inch lengths, and simmered in stews until tender. Try mashed parsnips: Peel and simmer in water until tender, and then purée them in a food processor or by forcing them through a food mill. Season with salt, pepper, and butter.

RUTABAGA

SWEET POTATO

PARSNIP

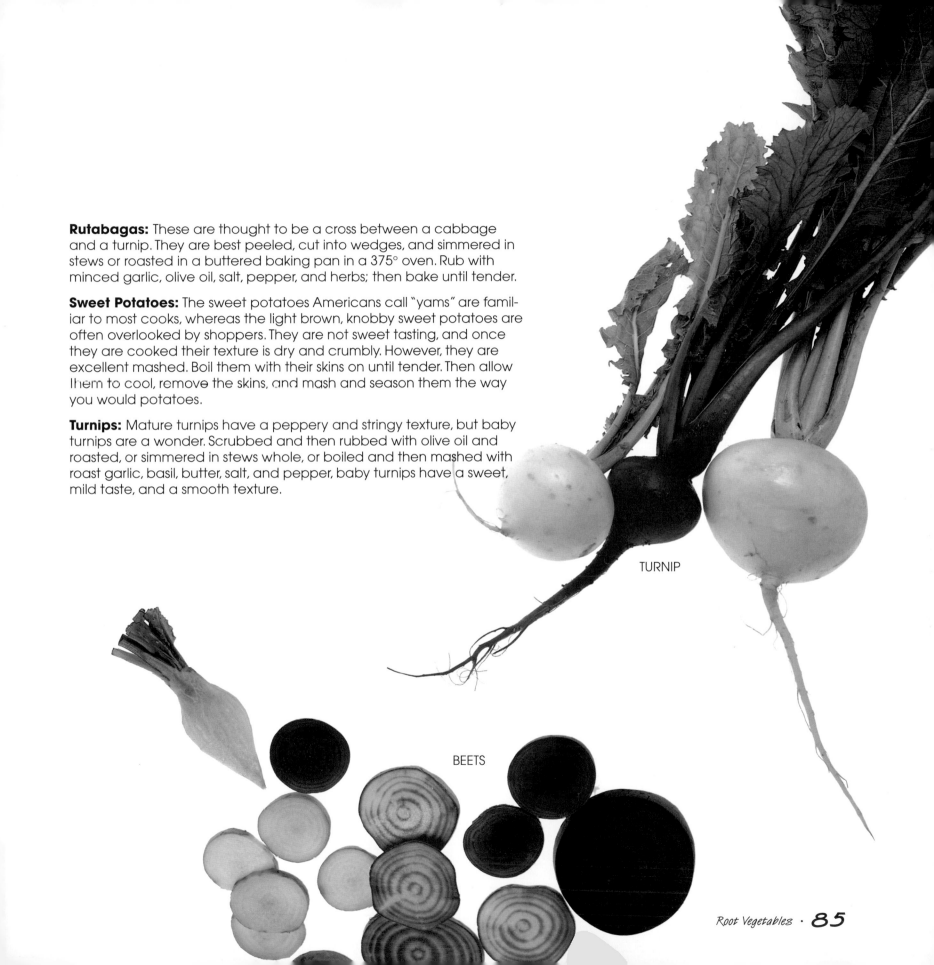

Rutabagas: These are thought to be a cross between a cabbage and a turnip. They are best peeled, cut into wedges, and simmered in stews or roasted in a buttered baking pan in a 375° oven. Rub with minced garlic, olive oil, salt, pepper, and herbs; then bake until tender.

Sweet Potatoes: The sweet potatoes Americans call "yams" are familiar to most cooks, whereas the light brown, knobby sweet potatoes are often overlooked by shoppers. They are not sweet tasting, and once they are cooked their texture is dry and crumbly. However, they are excellent mashed. Boil them with their skins on until tender. Then allow them to cool, remove the skins, and mash and season them the way you would potatoes.

Turnips: Mature turnips have a peppery and stringy texture, but baby turnips are a wonder. Scrubbed and then rubbed with olive oil and roasted, or simmered in stews whole, or boiled and then mashed with roast garlic, basil, butter, salt, and pepper, baby turnips have a sweet, mild taste, and a smooth texture.

TURNIP

BEETS

now peas, also called "pea pods," "Chinese pea pods," "Chinese sugar peas," and by the French **"mange tout"** ("eat it all"), need to be picked small, bought when very fresh, and cooked so briefly that their flat sides barely touch the wok. Always pick the smallest snow peas because the larger ones taste tough. To rescue snow peas that have begun to soften, submerge them for 5 minutes in ice water. Then pat them dry and stir-fry. This recipe, which takes only minutes to prepare and seconds to cook, combines snow peas with sugar snap peas and English peas. If buying the English peas at a market, give them a preliminary blanching as described in the recipe directions, so that during the wok cooking all the peas become cooked at the same time. As a possible menu, accompany this dish with shrimp louis salad with jumbo croutons, and candied bananas with ice cream.

Stir-Fried Snow Peas with Ginger-Butter Glaze

Serves 4 as a side dish

INGREDIENTS

3 cups snow peas

2 cups sugar snap peas

1 cup shelled English peas, about 2 pounds when in the pod

2 tablespoons flavorless cooking oil

2 tablespoons finely minced ginger

¼ cup vegetable broth

3 tablespoons Chinese rice wine or dry sherry

1 tablespoon oyster sauce

2 teaspoons dark sesame oil

2 teaspoons cornstarch

¼ teaspoon sugar

¼ teaspoon freshly ground black pepper

1 tablespoon unsalted butter, room temperature

ADVANCE PREPARATION

Snap the stem end off each snow pea pod, pulling away the fiber that runs along the top ridge. Combine the snow peas and sugar snap peas. Shell the English peas. If using English peas bought at the supermarket, blanch the peas; if using freshly harvested peas, skip this step. Bring 6 cups of water to a boil in a saucepan. Add the English peas. The moment they turn bright green, tip them into a sieve and immediately transfer them to a bowl filled with ice and cold water. After a few minutes chilling, re-move the English peas from the water and pat dry with paper towels. Combine them with the snow peas and sugar snap peas, and refrigerate. Combine the oil and ginger. In a small bowl, com-bine the broth, rice wine, oyster sauce, sesame oil, cornstarch, sugar, and pep-per. Set aside the butter at room tem-perature. *All advance preparation steps may be completed up to 8 hours before you begin the final steps.*

FINAL STEPS

Place a 14- to 16-inch flat-bottom wok or 12-inch sauté pan over highest heat. When the wok becomes very hot, add the oil and ginger to the center. Roll the oil around the wok, and when the ginger sizzles but has not turned brown, add the snow peas, sugar snap peas, and English peas. Stir and toss until the snow peas turn bright green, about 1 minute. Add the broth mixture. Bring to a low boil. Remove the wok from the heat, and stir in the butter. Immediately transfer to a heated serving platter or dinner plates and serve at once.

In this recipe, a large amount of spinach is blanched in boiling water, and then chopped finely and combined with shiitake mushrooms and goat cheese into a dumpling filling. Be sure to remove the spinach from the boiling water the moment it wilts, and to immediately rinse it under cold water, because otherwise the spinach will acquire a disagreeable color and have an overcooked taste. If you feel extravagant, double the amount of shiitake mushrooms and reduce the spinach by half. As a possible menu, accompany this dish with an heirloom beet salad, pumpkin soup, and almond tart.

Spinach Pot-Stickers

Serves 6 to 8 as an appetizer or 2 to 4 as an entrée

INGREDIENTS

2 to 3 ounces fresh shiitake mushrooms

2 cloves garlic, finely minced

1 tablespoon finely minced ginger

2 tablespoons flavorless cooking oil

3 bunches spinach (1½ pounds with stems on, about 10 to 12 cups of leaves, loosely packed)

¼ cup minced green onion

¼ cup soft goat cheese

½ teaspoon salt

¼ teaspoon freshly ground black pepper

36 round wonton skins

⅓ cup cornstarch

2 tablespoons flavorless cooking oil

SAUCE

½ cup chopped roasted red pepper

Corn kernels from 1 ear white corn

¼ cup chopped cilantro sprigs

1 clove garlic, finely minced

½ cup heavy cream

¼ cup dry vermouth or dry sherry

1 tablespoon oyster sauce

½ teaspoon Asian chile sauce

ADVANCE PREPARATION

Cut off and discard the mushroom stems. Cut the caps into shreds. Combine the garlic, ginger, and oil. Place a small sauté pan over medium-high heat. Add the oil mixture, and when it becomes hot, add the mushrooms. Stir and toss the mushrooms until they wilt, then tip into a bowl, and cool to room temperature.

To quickly stem spinach, do not remove the banding holding the stems together. Hold the bunch of spinach by the stems over a large bowl, and cut off the leaves so they fall into the bowl. Fill the bowl with cold water and vigorously stir the leaves. Bring only ¼ inch of water to a boil in a large saucepan, then transfer the spinach leaves from the bowl into the boiling water. Immediately turn the spinach with tongs. The moment the spinach wilts (this takes only seconds), tip the spinach into a colander. Rinse the spinach with cold water. Then, using your hands, press out all the moisture. Finish by chopping the spinach in a food processor. In the bowl holding the mushrooms, add the spinach, green onion, goat cheese, salt, and pepper. Mix well. Set aside separately the cornstarch and the cooking oil. In a bowl, combine the sauce and refrigerate.

Stack the wontons and cut into 3-inch-diameter circles. Place 2 teaspoons of the filling in the center of a round wonton wrapper. Bring the edges of the wonton up around the filling and encircle the pot-sticker "waist" with your index finger and thumb. Squeeze the waist gently with that same index finger, while also pressing the top and the bottom of the pot-sticker with your other index finger and thumb. Line a baking sheet with parchment paper and dust it heavily with cornstarch, place the pot-stickers in a single layer on the baking sheet, and refrigerate uncovered. *All advance preparation steps may be completed up to 8 hours before you begin the final steps.*

FINAL STEPS

Place a 12-inch nonstick saucepan over high heat. Add the cooking oil and immediately add the pot-stickers, bottom side down. Fry the pot-stickers until the bottoms become dark golden, about 2 minutes. Pour in the sauce. Immediately cover the pan, reduce the heat to medium, and steam the pot-stickers for 30 seconds. Remove the lid and shake the pan so that the pot-stickers "capsize" and are glazed all over with the sauce. Tip out onto a heated serving platter and serve at once.

S pinach or any tender leafy greens can be stir-fried. But the challenge to the cook is being able to stir-fry them without turning them into soup. Because the spinach cooks in seconds, it is tossed with the seasonings just prior to stir-frying. Other greens to cook this way are bok choy leaves, Bibb lettuce, or any other tender, leafy greens. As a possible menu, accompany this dish with grilled swordfish, tricolor tomato salad, and fresh berries with chocolate truffles.

Wok-Seared Spinach

Serves 4 as a side dish

INGREDIENTS

2 bunches spinach (about 1 pound with stems)

2 tablespoons flavorless cooking oil

2 tablespoons thin soy sauce

1 tablespoon dark sesame oil

½ teaspoon sugar

¼ teaspoon crushed red chile

3 cloves garlic, finely minced

1 tablespoon finely minced ginger

1 teaspoon grated or finely minced orange skin

¼ cup chopped green onion, chives, or cilantro sprigs

ADVANCE PREPARATION

Stem, wash, and spin dry the spinach using a lettuce spinner; refrigerate. In a small bowl, combine all the remaining ingredients. Stir well, and refrigerate. *All advance preparation steps may be completed up to 8 hours before you begin the final steps.*

FINAL STEPS

Place the spinach in a large bowl. Stir the seasoning mix, and then pour over the spinach. Toss the spinach leaves with your hands so that the leaves are evenly coated with the seasonings.

Place a 14- to 16-inch wok over highest heat. When the wok becomes very hot, add all the spinach. Toss the spinach quickly and evenly. The moment the spinach just begins to wilt (but with some of the leaves still not completely wilted), immediately transfer the spinach to a heated serving platter or heated dinner plates. Serve at once.

Mung beans are grown in a temperature-controlled environment and sprayed with mist periodically over 3 days until they sprout. Because of the clean growing conditions, never wash sprouts. Washing sprouts causes them to immediately lose their alluring crisp texture. If the sprouts at the market have any brown ends and don't feel rigid, they're not fresh enough to warrant purchasing. This very simple salad makes a great appetizer or a salad served with a substantial soup or with grilled meat. The combination of the crunchy bean sprouts (in Chinese called "vegetable for the teeth") and toasted almonds with the sweet, spicy, citrus dressing creates exciting taste and textural contrasts. As a possible menu, accompany this dish with crab and asparagus soup, corn muffins with honey butter, and a peach mousse.

Sprout Salad with Hot Wok Dressing

Serves 4 as a side dish

INGREDIENTS

8 cups bean sprouts

1 cup slivered almonds

3 tablespoons flavorless cooking oil

3 tablespoons finely minced ginger

1 teaspoon grated or finely minced orange zest

¼ cup Japanese rice vinegar, unseasoned

2 tablespoons light brown sugar

2 tablespoons thin soy sauce

1 tablespoon dark sesame oil

½ teaspoon Asian chile sauce

⅓ cup combined chopped mint and basil leaves

ADVANCE PREPARATION

Do not wash the sprouts; keep refrigerated. Preheat the oven to 325°. When it is preheated, toast the almonds on a baking sheet until golden, about 15 minutes. In a small bowl, combine the cooking oil, ginger, and orange zest. In a separate bowl, combine all the remaining ingredients except the herbs. *All advance preparation steps may be completed up to 8 hours before you begin the final steps.*

FINAL STEPS

Chop the mint and basil. Place the bean sprouts in a large bowl and scatter the herbs and almonds over the sprouts. Place a wok or sauté pan over highest heat. When the wok is very hot, add the oil-ginger mixture. Sauté briefly. Just before the ginger begins to brown, add the rice vinegar mixture. Bring to a low boil. Immediately pour the hot dressing over the sprouts. Using tongs, immediately toss the sprouts until evenly coated with the dressing. Transfer the salad to plates and serve at once.

uch is the profusion of winter and summer squash varieties that we cannot begin to picture and discuss the astounding shapes, gigantic sizes, and rich colors of those found each summer and fall at local farmers' markets. If you're a gardener, send away for some of the heirloom varieties. Just catching sight of winter squash partially hidden under its huge leaves will cause a smile. When choosing winter squash, the general rule is that for pies or cakes, squash with dry flesh is best; if planning to mash, stir-fry, stuff, place in soups, or fill with savory fillings and soups, choose moist-fleshed squash. As for summer squash, few other vegetables lend themselves to so many cooking techniques with such ease of preparation. Its delicate flavor makes it a perfect match for an outstanding range of seasonings, marinades, and sauces.

Winter and Summer Squash

Acorn Squash: Small, oval, and deeply indented, acorn squash is best cut in half and baked in a 375° oven. Just cut it in half, scrape away the interior seeds and fiber, brush the hollows with melted butter, grated nutmeg, salt, and pepper, and bake in the oven until tender, 45 minutes to 1 hour. Or make the fruit filling from the recipe on page 93.

Butternut Squash: These are cylindrical squash with yellow skin and flesh, bulging at one end, and weighing 2 to 3 pounds. The flesh is delicious baked, steamed, or simmered in soups and stews.

Hubbard Squash: These can be huge, and so are often sold cut into smaller pieces. The yellow orange flesh hiding under the green to bright orange skin is grainy, so it is best mashed or puréed.

Pumpkin: Beloved by the early American colonists, pumpkins can grow to hundreds of pounds. Buy small ones, which are more tender and flavorful, and use them for pie fillings, mashing, and as a vessel to hold soups.

Spaghetti Squash: This squash, which is shaped like a watermelon and weighs 4 to 8 pounds, is amazingly fun to cook. When cooked, the flesh separates into yellow-golden spaghetti-like strands. Bake the whole squash until the flesh is tender, then scrape the strands from the skin and serve with butter, salt, and pepper, or with any pasta sauce.

Summer Squash: Summer squash is good stir-fried, sautéed, stuffed and roasted in the oven, grilled, steamed, or cut into thin slices and eaten raw in salads. Experiment!

The preparation for this recipe takes about 30 minutes, but the last-minute cooking requires almost no attention. The stuffed acorn squash is great as a vegetarian entrée served between a soup course and salad. For a variation, reheat the stuffing in the microwave oven and serve it with grilled chicken or pork. As a possible menu, accompany this dish with a salad of garden greens.

Acorn Squash Stuffed with Dried Fruit and Grand Marnier

Serves 4 as an entrée

INGREDIENTS

2 acorn squash

3 tablespoons unsalted butter

2 tablespoons finely minced ginger

1 large apple, cored and diced

¼ cup dried currants or dark raisins

10 dried apricots, chopped

6 dried figs, chopped

¼ cup Grand Marnier

¼ cup white wine or water

2 tablespoons light brown sugar

1 teaspoon grated orange zest

Juice from 1 orange

½ teaspoon Asian chile sauce

¼ teaspoon ground cinnamon

ADVANCE PREPARATION

Cut 2 acorn squash in half across their waists; scrape away all the seeds and fiber. Cut a little of each end away so that later you will be able to stand the squash upright. Place a 12-inch sauté pan over medium-high heat. Add the butter and ginger. When the ginger sizzles, add the diced apple. Sauté until the apple softens. Then add the currants and all the remaining ingredients. Bring to a boil, cover, and simmer until all the liquid evaporates, about 4 minutes. Then cool the mixture. *All advance preparation steps may be completed up to 8 hours before you begin the final steps.*

FINAL STEPS

Preheat the oven to 375°. Approximately 1 hour prior to serving the dish, place ¼ inch of water in a baking dish, place the squash, hollow side down, in the water, and bake in the preheated oven for 40 minutes. Remove the squash from the oven. Drain away the water. Place each squash, hollow side up, in the baking dish. Place the fruit filling in the hollow sections. (It will only fill each acorn squash about halfway.) Return the squash to the oven and bake another 15 minutes until the squash becomes tender and the filling is piping hot. Serve at once.

In this recipe, summer squash is simmered in an easy-to-make and intensely flavored herb cream sauce. Try substituting button or shiitake mushrooms or asparagus for the squash. Or cook the sauce in a small saucepan and then toss it with 8 ounces boiled and drained pasta. As a possible menu, accompany this dish with grilled salmon, wild rice, and chocolate meltdown cookies.

Sautéed Summer Squash in Asian-Creole Cream Essence

Serves 4 to 6 as an entrée

INGREDIENTS

- **1 pound summer squash**
- **1 tablespoon unsalted butter**
- **2 tablespoons olive oil**
- **3 cloves garlic, finely minced**
- **2 vine-ripe tomatoes, seeded and chopped**
- **⅓ cup heavy cream**
- **¼ cup dry vermouth or dry sherry**
- **2 tablespoons oyster sauce**
- **1 teaspoon Asian chile sauce**
- **1 teaspoon sugar**
- **1 teaspoon cornstarch**
- **1 tablespoon chopped oregano leaves**
- **1 teaspoon chopped thyme leaves**

ADVANCE PREPARATION

Use one or any combination of summer squash. You will need 4 cups summer squash cut into ¼-inch-wide slices, each 1 to 4 inches in length. In a small bowl, combine butter, olive oil, and garlic. In another bowl, combine 2 vine-ripe tomatoes with all the remaining ingredients. *All advance preparation steps may be completed up to 8 hours before you begin the final steps.*

FINAL STEPS

Place a 12-inch sauté pan over high heat. When the pan is hot, add the butter-garlic mixture. When the butter melts and the garlic sizzles but has not turned brown, add the summer squash. Stir and toss, cooking on both sides until the summer squash brightens. Stir the sauce and then pour it into the sauté pan. Bring the sauce to a rapid boil. As soon as the sauce thickens into a glaze (about 30 seconds), transfer the summer squash and its sauce to a heated platter or dinner plates. Serve at once.

arinate summer squash for only a few minutes, because longer marinating causes it to soften too much. We like to set aside some of the marinade and then spoon it over the cooked squash just before serving to heighten the squash's flavors. This marinade is also great brushed across other grilled vegetables, and as a marinade for seafood and poultry. As a possible menu, accompany this with hamburgers, potato salad, and peach ice cream.

Grilled Summer Squash
Serves 4 to 6 as an entrée

INGREDIENTS
2 pounds summer squash
½ cup extra virgin olive oil
½ cup dry vermouth or dry sherry
½ cup thin soy sauce
½ cup honey
¼ cup oyster sauce
1 tablespoon Asian chile sauce
4 cloves garlic, finely minced
2 tablespoons finely minced ginger
Zest from 2 limes, grated, plus the juice
½ cup combination fresh cilantro, mint, and basil

ADVANCE PREPARATION

Cut squash into ¼-inch-wide strips. In a bowl, combine all the remaining ingredients. Stir to evenly combine. *All advance preparation steps may be completed up to 8 hours before you begin the final steps.*

FINAL STEPS

Prepare a wood or charcoal fire in the barbecue, or preheat a gas grill to medium. Pour the marinade over the squash and toss to evenly combine. When the coals are ash-colored or the gas grill has been preheated, brush the cooking grate with oil, and grill the summer squash. The squash should sizzle as you lay it on the grill. Cook until the summer squash softens slightly and acquires grill marks, about 2 minutes on each side. Serve at once, accompanied by any extra marinade so people can drizzle this over the grilled squash.

moking tomatoes over a gas or charcoal fire contributes a deep, earthy flavor that lingers after the last bite. You will need about ¹/₄ cup hardwood chips. Place them on a layer of foil over the gas flames and heat them until they begin to smoke. Then add the tomatoes. Or, if using charcoal or a wood fire, scatter the wood chips across the coals and add the tomatoes immediately. Any type of firm tomato, when smoked, adds a great additional flavor to tomato sauces, salsas, tomato soups, and pizza sauces. As a possible menu, accompany this dish with fava bean salad and candied pineapple tart.

Smoked Tomatoes Tossed with Fusilli Pasta

Serves 4 as a side dish or 2 as an entrée

INGREDIENTS

3 pounds vine-ripe Roma tomatoes

2 tablespoons extra virgin olive oil

2 tablespoons finely minced ginger

4 cloves garlic, finely minced

¹/₂ cup unsweetened coconut milk

¹/₂ cup vegetable or chicken broth

¹/₄ cup Chinese rice wine or dry sherry

2 tablespoons oyster sauce

2 tablespoons dark sesame oil

2 teaspoons Asian chile sauce

¹/₂ cup chopped basil leaves

1 cup freshly grated imported Parmesan cheese

8 ounces dried fusilli or your favorite pasta

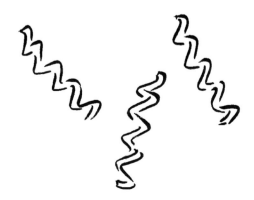

ADVANCE PREPARATION

Preheat a gas grill to medium, or prepare a charcoal fire. Cut each tomato in half. When the gas grill is hot, place the wood chips on a small layer of aluminum foil and place in the corner of the cooking grate. When the chips begin to smoke, brush the grate with oil. Place the tomatoes on the cooking grate and cover the grill. If using coals, when they have turned ash-colored, scatter on the wood chips, add the tomatoes, and cover the grill. Grill the tomatoes on both sides until they soften slightly and become lightly charred, about 5 minutes. Transfer the tomatoes to a colander and let drain 20 minutes. After 20 minutes, if the skin is tough, discard. Then chop the tomatoes coarsely without removing the seeds.

In a small bowl, combine oil, ginger, and garlic and set aside. In another small bowl, combine coconut milk, broth, rice wine, oyster sauce, sesame oil, chile sauce, and basil. Stir the chopped tomatoes into the sauce, and refrigerate. Set aside cheese and pasta. *All advance preparation steps may be completed up to 8 hours before you begin the final steps.*

FINAL STEPS

Bring 4 quarts of water to a rapid boil. Lightly salt the water, then cook the pasta according to the instructions on the package. When the pasta loses its raw texture but is still slightly firm, remove from the heat and drain.

Return the empty pasta pot to the stove over high heat. Wipe the pan with a clean towel. Then add the oil, ginger, and garlic. Sauté for a few seconds and add the tomato sauce and bring to a boil. Immediately stir in the pasta. Stir until evenly combined. Taste and adjust the seasonings. Transfer the pasta to a heated serving platter or heated dinner plates. Sprinkle with cheese and serve at once.

One of our favorite Napa Valley restaurants is Jan Birnbaum's Catahoula Restaurant, located in Calistoga. In the summer he serves an amazing tomato salad, and we have tried to duplicate the recipe here. This dish is an array of vine-ripe tomatoes sliced thickly, smaller slices of tomatoes grilled or smoked, unripe green tomatoes battered and fried, and whole cherry tomatoes all arranged into a riot of colors, textures, and flavors. Accented by a balsamic vinegar dressing and sprigs of peppery watercress, this recipe highlights tomatoes in all their glory. As a possible menu, accompany this dish with chilled asparagus and shellfish soup, garlic bread sprinkled with Parmesan, and chocolate soufflés with berry sauce.

Tomatoes in All Their Glory

Serves 4 to 6 as a side dish

INGREDIENTS

4 large vine-ripe red or yellow tomatoes

4 medium vine-ripe tomatoes

1 tablespoon sugar

2 medium unripe green tomatoes

2 eggs, beaten

½ cup white flour

4 cups tender watercress

3 ounces soft goat cheese

32 cherry tomatoes

2 tablespoons flavorless cooking oil

DRESSING

½ cup extra virgin olive oil

6 tablespoons balsamic vinegar

2 tablespoons thin soy sauce

1 tablespoon Asian chile sauce

2 tablespoons finely minced ginger

1 small garlic clove, finely minced

¼ cup chopped cilantro sprigs

ADVANCE PREPARATION

Cut each large tomato into 3 thick slices; set aside. Cut each medium vine-ripe tomato into 3 slices; sprinkle the slices on both sides with a little sugar and set aside. Cut each medium unripe tomato into 3 slices. Then dip each slice of the unripe tomatoes on both sides into the beaten egg, and lightly coat them with flour. Transfer to a wire rack and refrigerate. Prepare the watercress and refrigerate. Crumble the goat cheese and refrigerate. Set aside the cherry tomatoes. In a small bowl, combine the oil, vinegar, soy sauce, chile sauce, ginger, garlic, and cilantro; refrigerate. *All advance preparation steps may be completed up to 8 hours before you begin the final steps.*

FINAL STEPS

Prepare a charcoal fire, or preheat a gas barbecue to medium, or preheat an indoor grill pan. When hot, grill the medium vine-ripe tomatoes on both sides until lightly charred, then set aside temporarily. Place a 12-inch sauté pan over medium-high heat. When the pan is hot, add the cooking oil. When the oil gives off just a wisp of smoke, fry the breaded tomato slices until golden on both sides; then drain on a wire rack.

Place the large tomato slices on dinner plates. Add layers of grilled and breaded tomatoes, separated by sprigs of watercress. Scatter the cherry tomatoes around the edges of the large tomatoes. Stir the salad dressing, and drizzle the dressing over the tomatoes. Sprinkle on the goat cheese. Serve at once.

Tomato Salsas

Quick Tomato Salsa

Makes 2 cups

1½ cups seeded and chopped vine-ripe tomatoes

¼ cup chopped cilantro sprigs

2 cloves garlic, finely minced

Juice from 1 lime

1 tablespoon light brown sugar

1 tablespoon Asian chile sauce

¼ teaspoon salt

Combine all the ingredients, and set aside at room temperature.

Thai-Inspired Tomato Salsa

Makes 2½ cups

1½ cups seeded and chopped vine-ripe tomatoes

½ cup chopped cilantro sprigs

¼ cup chopped green onions

1 tablespoon finely minced ginger

3 tablespoons freshly squeezed lime juice

2 tablespoons light brown sugar

2 tablespoons Thai or Vietnamese fish sauce

2 teaspoons Thai or other Asian chile sauce

Combine all the ingredients, and set aside at room temperature.

Green Tomato and Banana Salsa

Makes 3 cups

1 firm banana

1 cup seeded and chopped green tomatoes

2 cloves finely minced garlic

3 fresh serrano chiles, finely minced with seeds

2 tablespoons chopped mint leaves

2 tablespoons chopped cilantro sprigs

2 tablespoons freshly squeezed lime juice

2 tablespoons freshly squeezed orange juice

2 tablespoons light brown sugar

¼ teaspoon ground allspice

Peel the banana and cut it in half lengthwise. Then cut it crosswise into the thinnest possible pieces. Transfer to a bowl. Add all the remaining ingredients. If not using within 1 hour, then press plastic wrap across the surface of the salsa and refrigerate. Use the same day it's made.

Chinese Salsa

Makes 4 cups

4 dried shiitake mushrooms (forest mushrooms)

2 cups seeded and chopped vine-ripe tomatoes

½ cup chopped green onion

¼ cup chopped cilantro sprigs

2 cloves garlic, finely minced

2 tablespoons finely minced ginger

3 tablespoons red or white wine vinegar

2 tablespoons dark sesame oil

1½ tablespoons sugar

1 tablespoon safflower oil

1 tablespoon thin soy sauce

2 teaspoons Asian chile sauce

Cover the mushrooms with very hot tap water. When soft, about 20 minutes, discard the stems, and chop the mushrooms. In a bowl, combine the chopped mushrooms with all the remaining ingredients. Stir to evenly combine. Set aside at room temperature.

The crisp, slightly peppery taste of watercress makes it a perfect "palate cleanser." It's particularly good matched with sweet orange slices and hot slices of goat cheese just removed from the broiler. Because watercress is fragile, try to purchase and use it on the same day. Using your fingers, snap off the tender ends, immerse them in cold water, and refrigerate. This way the watercress will stay at the peak of freshness. As a possible menu, accompany this dish with wild rice gumbo, homemade potato fries, and Grand Marnier chocolate ice cream.

Watercress with Orange Segments and Warm Goat Cheese

Serves 4 as a salad and 2 as an entrée

INGREDIENTS

6 cups watercress

2 small oranges

6 ounces soft goat cheese, chilled

½ cup unseasoned bread crumbs

1 cup raw walnut halves

DRESSING

1 teaspoon grated or finely minced orange zest

2 tablespoons freshly squeezed orange juice

2 tablespoons safflower oil

2 tablespoons white or red wine vinegar

1 tablespoon thin soy sauce

1 teaspoon honey

1 teaspoon Asian chile sauce

2 tablespoons finely minced fresh ginger

1 small clove garlic, finely minced

2 tablespoons minced cilantro sprigs

ADVANCE PREPARATION

Preheat the oven to 325°. Wash watercress, discard tough stems, and refrigerate immersed in cold water. Peel and cut the oranges into segments; refrigerate. Cut the goat cheese in 8 or 12 pieces. Using bread crumbs, dust each goat cheese slice on the top and sides, but not on the bottom, and refrigerate. Place the walnuts on a baking sheet and toast in the preheated oven for 15 minutes. Then cool to room temperature. In a jar, combine the ingredients for the dressing. *All advance preparation steps may be completed up to 8 hours before you begin the final steps.*

FINAL STEPS

Turn the oven to broil and preheat for 10 minutes. Drain and pat dry the watercress. Place the watercress and orange slices in a bowl. Shake the dressing, then add half the salad dressing to the watercress and orange slices, and toss gently. Arrange the watercress and oranges on salad or dinner plates. Place the cheese with the bread crumb tops facing upwards on a baking sheet. Place the baking sheet 4 inches below the broiler and broil the cheese on only one side for 1 to 2 minutes, until the cheese has just been warmed and the bread crumbs brown lightly. Place 2 or 3 slices of the goat cheese in the center of each salad. Add the walnuts. Drizzle any remaining salad dressing over the goat cheese. Alternatively, overlap the watercress, orange slices, and goat cheese; then sprinkle on the salad dressing. Serve at once.

rue yams, which are originally from Africa and are rarely found in the United States, have white flesh, a barklike skin, and can weigh over 100 pounds. The "Louisiana yams," or just "yams" sold in our markets, are yellow sweet potatoes. This large edible root, belonging to the morning-glory family, is native to the Caribbean. You will find both the pale-skinned variety, usually correctly labeled "sweet potato," and the red-skinned type with yellow flesh at every supermarket. For this recipe you should purchase the latter, because it has a better texture and is far sweeter when roasted. These "yams," or, for that matter, potatoes, parsnips, turnips, and carrots, can be rubbed with the flavored oil provided in this recipe and then roasted in a hot oven until tender and crisp, making an easy and satisfying side dish. For flavor variation, replace the mint and cilantro with chopped rosemary. As a possible menu, accompany this dish with barbecued game hens flavored with chiles, goat cheese and watercress salad, and apricot crisp.

Yams with Orange, Cinnamon, and Chile

Serves 4 as a side dish

INGREDIENTS

3 pounds yams

⅓ cup extra virgin olive oil

6 cloves garlic, finely minced

¼ cup finely minced ginger

2 teaspoons grated or finely minced orange zest

1 teaspoon Asian chile sauce or crushed red chile

1 teaspoon salt

½ teaspoon ground allspice

¼ cup mixture chopped mint leaves and cilantro sprigs

ADVANCE PREPARATION

Peel the yams. Cut them into ½-inch slices; then cut each slice into strips. Place the strips together and cut across them to make ½-inch cubes. You should have approximately 10 cups. Refrigerate the yams until ready to roast. In a small bowl, combine the oil, garlic, ginger, orange zest, chile sauce, salt, and allspice. *All advance preparation steps may be completed up to 8 hours before you begin the final steps.*

FINAL STEPS

Preheat the oven to 400°. Chop the mint and cilantro. Place the yams in a large bowl. Stir the oil mixture, and then pour it over the yams. Stir the yams until evenly coated. Spray a wire rack with nonstick spray. Place the wire rack on a baking pan lined with foil, scatter the yams in a single layer across the wire rack, and place the baking sheet in the oven. Roast until the yams can be easily pierced with a fork, approximately 30 minutes. Sprinkle with mint and cilantro. Serve at once.

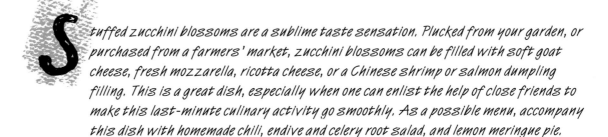

S tuffed zucchini blossoms are a sublime taste sensation. Plucked from your garden, or purchased from a farmers' market, zucchini blossoms can be filled with soft goat cheese, fresh mozzarella, ricotta cheese, or a Chinese shrimp or salmon dumpling filling. This is a great dish, especially when one can enlist the help of close friends to make this last-minute culinary activity go smoothly. As a possible menu, accompany this dish with homemade chili, endive and celery root salad, and lemon meringue pie.

Zucchini Blossoms Stuffed with Goat Cheese
Serves 4 as a side dish

INGREDIENTS

8 small zucchini blossoms

1 red bell pepper

¼ cup chopped parsley or cilantro sprigs

2 cloves garlic, finely minced

2 tablespoons finely minced ginger

½ teaspoon salt

¼ teaspoon Asian chile sauce or ground black pepper

6 ounces soft goat cheese

3 eggs, well beaten

1 cup all-purpose white flour

1 cup flavorless cooking oil

ADVANCE PREPARATION

Remove and discard the centers from the zucchini blossoms. Char the red pepper by placing it directly over a gas stove-top burner turned to high. When the pepper blackens on the underside, rotate the pepper one-third turn, and continue charring the pepper until it is entirely blackened. Or blacken the pepper under the electric oven broiler coil by placing it on the oven rack about 5 inches from the broiler coil. Once the pepper is blackened, place it in a paper or plastic bag, and twist the top closed; after 5 minutes rub away the charred skin. Now seed, stem, and chop the pepper.

In a bowl, combine the pepper, parsley, garlic, ginger, salt, chile sauce, and cheese. Using your fingers, evenly mix the ingredients. Stuff the blossoms, and refrigerate. *All advance preparation steps may be completed up to 8 hours before you begin the final steps.*

FINAL STEPS

Beat the eggs. Set aside the flour on a large piece of wax paper or newspaper. Gently dip a blossom in the egg and then turn the blossom in the flour. Shake off excess flour and transfer the blossom to a wire rack. Repeat with the remaining blossoms.

Heat the oil in a 12-inch sauté pan over medium-high heat. The oil is at the right temperature when bubbles come from the end of a wooden spoon when placed in the oil (350 to 365°). Fry about 6 to 8 blossoms at a time in the oil. Cook on both sides until they turn golden, about 4 minutes total cooking time. Transfer the cooked blossoms back to the wire rack, and fry the remaining blossoms. Pat with paper towels. Transfer the blossoms to heated appetizer or dinner plates. Serve at once.

The best method for cooking stuffed zucchini is to first bake it in order to cook the zucchini, and then finish by broiling the stuffed zucchini so that both its top surface and the filling acquire an attractive golden hue. The shiitake mushroom and cheese filling is also very good as a stuffing for zucchini blossoms or as a vegetarian filling for tortellini and Chinese dumplings. As a possible menu, accompany this dish with grilled rosemary chicken, mango-ginger salad, and strawberries jubilee.

Zucchini Stuffed with Shiitake Mushrooms

Serves 6 to 8 as a side dish or 2 to 4 as an entrée

INGREDIENTS

4 medium zucchini, 1 pound total
2 tablespoons extra virgin olive oil
2 tablespoons unsalted butter
2 cloves garlic, finely minced
¼ pound fresh shiitake mushrooms
2 small whole green onions
3 tablespoons soft goat cheese
¼ cup grated Gruyère cheese
Salt and freshly ground black pepper to taste

SALSA
Choose a salsa from page 99.

ADVANCE PREPARATION

Do not cut off the zucchini ends. Cut the zucchini in half lengthwise. Using a small spoon, scrape away the seeds, forming a long hollow running down the center of each zucchini. Rub the cut surface (but not the hollowed-out sections) with olive oil. Combine the butter and garlic. Discard the shiitake stems, then cut the caps in ⅛-inch-wide slices. Mince the green onions. Place a 10-inch sauté pan over medium heat. Add the butter and garlic. When the garlic sizzles, add the shiitakes and onions. Sauté until the mushrooms wilt, about 3 minutes. Transfer to a bowl, and cool to room temperature. Then evenly mix in the cheese. Taste and season for salt and pepper. Place the filling in the hollowed section of each zucchini. If not cooking the zucchini within 30 minutes, then refrigerate.

Make the salsa, place in a small saucepan, and keep at room temperature. *All advance preparation steps may be completed up to 8 hours before you begin the final steps.*

FINAL STEPS

Preheat the oven to 375°. Place the zucchini, filling side up, on a baking sheet lined with cooking parchment paper or foil. Place 4 inches from the broiler in the preheated oven and bake until tender, about 15 minutes. Turn the oven setting to broil and cook until the filling browns, about 4 minutes.

Transfer the zucchini to a heated platter or dinner plates. Warm the salsa. Spoon the salsa across the zucchini so that the salsa forms a pool of sauce on each side of the zucchini. Serve at once.

Glossary

Cheese (Parmesan, Pecorino, and Asiago): Use these three cheeses interchangeably. Because the imported Italian cheeses have a far superior taste to the same type of cheese made in this country, make an extra effort to locate these Italian cheeses at upscale supermarkets and cheese shops. As long as the cheese has not been grated, it will last at least 1 month if wrapped airtight and refrigerated.

Chile Sauce, Asian: This is a general term for the countless varieties of chile sauces imported from Asia, which are added to provide "heat" to the food. Use your own favorite chile sauce and vary the amount depending on personal preference. Most of the recipes designate "Asian chile sauce." Best brand: "Rooster" Delicious Hot Chile Garlic Sauce, sold in 8-ounce clear plastic jars with a green cap. Refrigerate after opening. Substitute: One or more fresh jalapeño or serrano chiles.

Chiles, Ancho: These reddish-purple dried chiles have a fruity, mildly spicy taste that makes them a great addition, particularly to tomato sauces and homemade chili. They are sold in all Mexican markets and in American supermarkets that have a wide selection of dry chiles. Substitute: Dried mulato or pasilla chiles.

Chiles, Fresh: The smaller the chile, the spicier its taste. Over 80 percent of the "heat" is concentrated in the inside ribbing and seeds. Because it Is a tedious operation to remove the seeds from jalapeño and serrano chiles, we always mince the chiles with their seeds. If recipes specify seeding a small chile, just use half the amount of chiles, and mince the chiles with their seeds in an electric mini-chopper. Substitute: Your favorite bottled chile sauce.

Citrus Juice and Zest: Freshly squeezed citrus juice has a sparkling fresh taste completely absent in all store-bought juices. Because its flavor deteriorates quickly, always squeeze citrus juice within hours of use and keep refrigerated. Recipes that say "zested and finely minced" mean to remove the colored skin of the citrus using a simple tool called a zester (very easy to use) and then finely mince the zest rather than trying to scrape the citrus against the fine mesh of a cheese grater (very time-consuming).

Coconut Milk: Adds flavor and body to sauces. Always purchase a Thai brand whose ingredients are just coconut and water. Do not buy the new "low calorie" coconut milk, which has a terrible taste. Stir the coconut milk before using. Best brand: Chaokoh Brand from Thailand. Once opened, store coconut milk in the refrigerator for up to 1 week, then discard. Substitute: Half-and-half.

Cooking Oil, Flavorless: Use any flavorless oil that has a high smoking temperature, such as peanut oil, canola oil, safflower oil, and corn oil.

Crème Fraîche: This is a sour-tasting cream with nutty undertones. Look for it in the supermarket section where sour cream is displayed. You can also substitute sour cream.

Egg-Roll Skins: These are made from the same fresh pasta dough used for making wonton skins. Egg-roll skins are available fresh at most supermarkets, in either the deli or the produce area.

Fish Sauce, Thai or Vietnamese: Fish sauce, made from fermenting fish in brine, is used in Southeast Asian cooking in much the same way that the Chinese use soy sauce. Purchase Thai or Vietnamese fish sauce, which has the lowest salt content. Best brands: Three Crab, Phu Quoc Flying Lion, or Tiparos Fish Sauce. Substitute: Thin soy sauce, although the flavor is quite different.

Ginger Root, Fresh: These pungent and spicy "roots" are grown in Hawaii and are available at all supermarkets in the produce section. Buy firm ginger with a smooth skin. It is unnecessary to peel ginger unless the skin is wrinkled. To use: Because the tough ginger fiber runs lengthwise along the root, always cut the ginger crosswise in *paper-thin* slices, then *very finely mince* in an electric mini-chopper. Good-quality fresh ginger is now inexpensive and easily available. It is unnecessary to take elaborate storage precautions. There is no substitute for fresh ginger.

Hoisin Sauce: Hoisin sauce, a thick and sweet, spicy, dark condiment, is made with soy beans, chiles, garlic, ginger, and sugar. Once opened, it keeps indefinitely at room temperature. Best brand: Koon Chun Hoisin Sauce.

Kalamata Olives: Dark purple, rich, and fruity tasting, these and other dark olives from Europe are utterly different tasting and far superior to the dreadful American canned black olives. Kalamata olives and other varieties are now sold by many supermarkets and at all Mediterranean markets.

Olive Oil: Recipes specifying "extra virgin olive oil" benefit from the additional flavor of this intensely flavored oil. Recipes specifying just "olive oil" or "light olive oil" use this type of oil when little or no olive oil taste is desired.

Oyster Sauce: Also called "oyster-flavored sauce," this sauce gives dishes a rich taste without a hint of its seafood origins. Keeps indefinitely in the refrigerator. There is no substitute. Although it is available at every supermarket, the following best brands are available mostly at Asian markets: Sa Cheng Oyster Flavored Sauce, Hop Sing Lung Oyster Sauce, and Lee Kum Kee Oyster Flavored Sauce, Premium.

Rice Wine, Chinese, or Dry Sherry: Please note that we mean "rice wine" and never "rice vinegar"! Always use good-quality Chinese rice wine or an American or Spanish dry sherry. For rice wine, the best brands are Pagoda Shao Xing Rice Wine, Pagoda Shao Hsing Hua Tiao Chiew. You can also use a moderately expensive dry sherry or Japanese sake.

Sesame Oil, Dark: A nutty, dark golden brown oil made from toasted, crushed sesame seeds, dark sesame oil should not be confused with the American-manufactured clear-colored and tasteless sesame oil or Chinese black sesame oil, which has a strong, unpleasant taste. Dark sesame oil will last for at least a year at room temperature and indefinitely in the refrigerator. Best brand: Kadoya Sesame Oil.

Soy Sauce, Heavy: Heavy, "dark," or "black" soy sauce is slightly thicker (molasses or caramel is added) than thin soy sauce and has a richer flavor. Do not confuse heavy soy sauce with "thick" soy sauce, which is an overwhelmingly powerful-tasting syrup.

Soy Sauce, Thin: "Thin" or "light" soy sauce is a watery, mildly salty liquid made from soy beans, roasted wheat, yeast, and salt. If you are concerned about sodium, reduce the quantity of soy sauce rather than using the inferior-tasting, more expensive low-sodium brands. Best brands: Pearl River Bridge Golden Label Superior Soy Sauce, Koon Chun Thin Soy Sauce, or Kikkoman Regular Soy Sauce.

Tomatoes, Fresh, and Tomato Paste: All recipes using tomatoes specify "vine-ripe tomatoes." During the months when these are unavailable, substitute "hothouse tomatoes." To increase the flavor of hothouse tomatoes, cut the tomatoes into ¼-inch slices and broil or grill the tomatoes on both sides until lightly golden. This intensifies their tomato flavor. Then cut and use as directed in the recipe. In addition, we often add 1 teaspoon of tomato paste, of which a good brand is Pagani, sold in 4½-ounce tubes.

Vegetable Broth: There are very acceptable canned vegetable broths sold at every supermarket, or you can use the vegetable stock recipe at the beginning of the book. For a substitute, chicken broth works very well.

Vinegar, Balsamic: This vinegar has a nutty, mildly sour, slightly sweet flavor. For recipes in this book, use a moderately priced balsamic vinegar ($5 for an 8-ounce bottle) available in most supermarkets.

Vinegar, Rice: The mild flavor of Japanese rice vinegar makes this a great addition to salads. Avoid "seasoned" or "gourmet" rice vinegar, which has sugar and MSG added.

Artists' Credits

We would especially like to thank our artists. Ceramic artist Julie Cline of Oakland, California, made the handpainted dishes on pages 25, 42, 51, and 97. Susan Eslick of San Francisco provided the distinctive ceramics on pages 6-7, 26-27, 28, 75, and 78. Julie Sanders of the Cyclamen Collection, Emeryville, Calif., contributed her bold dishware on pages 1, 45, 48, 66, and 72. Viviana Lombrozo of Viviana/Art Studio in La Jolla, Calif., made the chargers/service plates on pages 68, 83, and 86. Kathy Erteman of New York City made the black and white ceramic vessels on page 33. M. Marin provided the chili platter on page 21. Thank you all for being part of **Hot Vegetables**.

Tantau Gallery, St. Helena, Calif., provided the ceramics by Barbara Eigen on page 37, the dishes by C. Sara and Barbara Eigen on page 61, the bowls by Heather Shadron on pages 81 and 109, and the dishes by Festin, Loquin, France, on page 100.

Fillamento Gallery, San Francisco, represents the Hogana's Keramic plates and Eastern Accent flatware on page 53, the flatware by Mekael Bjornstjerna for Sasaki on page 66, and the Sasaki plates on page 105. The Culinary Institute of America, Greystone, St. Helena, Calif., provided the cookware pictured on pages 18 and 79. Thank you all.

Acknowledgments

Many friends helped bring this book into print, and we deeply appreciate their support. Food stylist Carol Cole added beauty to many of the photos. Thank you Ten Speed Press, particularly Phil Wood, our publisher Kirsty Melville, editor Chelsea Vaughn, and Jo Ann Deck and Dennis Hayes in special sales. Our friend and book designer Beverly Wilson contributed her unique vision for the book. Jack and Dolores Cakebread provided their winery kitchen for testing many of these recipes, with a small group of cooking friends. All the recipes were developed using the superb Viking Range equipment and Calphalon Cookware.

Conversion Charts

LIQUID MEASUREMENTS

Cups and Spoons	Fluid Ounces	Approximate Metric Term	Approximate Centiliters	Actual Milliliters
1 tsp	⅙ oz	*	½ cL	5 mL
1 Tb	½ oz	*	1½ cL	15 mL
¼ c	2 oz	½ dL	6 cL	59 mL
⅓ c	2⅔ oz	¾ dL	8 cL	79 mL
½ c	4 oz	1 dL	12 cL	119 mL
⅔ c	5⅓ oz	1½ dL	15 cL	157 mL
¾ c	6 oz	1¾ dL	18 cL	178 mL
1 c	8 oz	¼ L	24 cL	237 mL
1¼ c	10 oz	3 dL	30 cL	296 mL
1⅓ c	10⅔ oz	3¼ dL	33 cL	325 mL
1½ c	12 oz	3½ dL	35 cL	355 mL
1⅔ c	13⅓ oz	3¾ dL	39 cL	385 mL
1¾ c	14 oz	4 dL	41 cL	414 mL
2 c; 1 pt	16 oz	½ L	47 cL	473 mL
2½ c	20 oz	6 dL	60 cL	592 mL
3 c	24 oz	¾ L	70 cL	710 mL
3½ c	28 oz	⅘ L	83 cL	829 mL
4 c	32 oz	1 L	95 cL	946 mL
5 c	40 oz	1¼ L	113 cL	1134 mL
6 c	48 oz	1½ L	142 cL	1420 mL
8 c	64 oz	2 L	190 cL	1893 mL
10 c	80 oz	2½ L	235 cL	2366 mL
12 c	96 oz	2¾ L	284 cL	2839 mL
4 qt	128 oz	3¾ L	375 cL	3785 mL
5 qt	160 oz			
6 qt	192 oz			
8 qt	256 oz			

* Metric equivalent too small for home measure.

LENGTH

⅛ in = 3 mm
¼ in = 6 mm
⅓ in = 1 cm
½ in = 1.5 cm
¾ in = 2 cm
1 in = 2.5 cm
1½ in – 4 cm
2 in = 5 cm
2½ in = 6 cm
4 in = 10 cm
8 in = 20 cm
10 in = 25 cm

TEMPERATURES

275°F = 140°C
300°F = 150°C
325°F = 170°C
350°F = 180°C
375°F = 190°C
400°F = 200°C
425°F = 215°C
450°F = 230°C
475°F = 240°C
500°F = 250°C

OTHER CONVERSIONS

Ounces to milliliters: multiply ounces by 29.57

Quarts to liters: multiply quarts by 0.95

Milliliters to ounces: multiply milliliters by 0.034

Liters to quarts: multiply liters by 1.057

Ounces to grams: multiply ounces by 28.3

Grams to ounces: multiply grams by .0353

Pounds to grams: multiply pounds by 453.59

Pounds to kilograms: multiply pounds by 0.45

Cups to liters: multiply cups by 0.24

Index

A

Acorn squash, 92
  Acorn Squash Stuffed with Dried Fruit and Grand
    Marnier, 93
Artichokes
  Artichoke and Roasted Red Pepper Tart, 20
  Steamed Artichokes with Spicy Asian Dipping
    Sauces, 22
Asian Dipping Sauces, 22
Asian Hollandaise Sauce, Brussels Sprouts with, 34
Asian vegetables, 58–59. *See also specific vegetables*
Asparagus, 11
  with Asian Hollandaise Sauce (substitute), 34
  Asparagus Mu Shu with Shiitake Mushrooms, 24
  Asparagus Salad with Pine Nuts, 23
  with Tofu and Shiitake Mushrooms (substitute), 31

B

Batters for deep-frying, 17
Beans. *See* Fava beans; Green beans; Lima beans;
  Long beans; Soybeans
Bean sprouts
  Sprout Salad with Hot Wok Dressing, 91
Beer Batter, 17
Beets, 11, 84
  Roasted Beet Salad with Fresh Mozzarella
    Cheese, 29
Blanching, 10, 15
Blue Cheese Dressing, 55
Bok choy, 58
  Stir-Fried Bok Choy with Mushrooms and
    Peppers, 30

Broccoli, 11
  with Asian Hollandaise Sauce (substitute), 34
  Broccoli with Tofu and Shiitake Mushrooms, 31
  Mu Shu with Shiitake Mushrooms (substitute), 24
  Wok-Seared Broccoli with Orange Sauce and
    Pine Nuts, 32
Broccoli, Chinese, 58
Broiling, 10–11
Broth, vegetable, 19, 107
Brussels sprouts with Asian Hollandaise Sauce, 34

C

Cabbage with Eggs, Chinese Black Beans, and
    Chiles, 35
Carrots, 11
  Carrot Risotto, 36
  with Orange, Cinnamon, and Chile (substitute), 102
Cauliflower, 11
  Stir-Fried Cauliflower with Mediterranean
    Accents, 38
Celery Root Soup with Ginger and Herbs, 39
Chile Croutons, 54
Chiles, 40
  Chile Mango Salsa, 40
  Chiles Rellenos, 41
Chinese Salsa, 99
Coconut Wok Sauce, 13
Conversion charts, 109
Corn, 11
  Corn Tamale Mousse, 44
  Thai Corn Soup with Chile-Jam Accent, 43
Cucumbers
  Cucumbers Pickled with Garlic and Chiles, 46
  Japanese, 58

D

Deep-frying, 16–17

E

Egg Batter, 17
Eggplant, 11
  Asian varieties, 59
  Grilled Eggplant Lasagna, 49
  Thai Eggplant Ratatouille, 47
Endive Salad with Candied Walnuts and
    Papaya Nests, 50

F

Fava beans, 26
Fennel Salad with Mango-Walnut Herb Dressing, 52

G

Ginger Herb Dressing, 55
Ginger-Soy Dressing, Green Bean Salad with, 56
Green beans, 11

Green Bean Salad with Ginger-Soy Dressing, 56
  Stir-Fried Szechwan Green Beans, 57
Green Tomato and Banana Salsa, 99
Grilling, roasting, and broiling, 10–11

I

Ingredients, glossary of, 106–107

J

Jicama Tex-Mex Salad, 60

K

Kale Sautéed with Garlic and Balsamic Vinegar, 62
Kohlrabi, 84

L

Lasagna, Grilled Eggplant, 49
Leek Timbale Towers, 63
Lemon Garlic Dressing, Creamy, 55
Lima beans, 26, 27
Long-cooking vs. short-cooking vegetables, 12

M

Mangoes
  Chile Mango Salsa, 40
  Fennel Salad with Mango-Walnut Herb Dressing, 52
Marinating, 10
Microwaving and pressure-cooking, 18
Mushrooms, 11
  Asparagus Mu Shu with Shiitake Mushrooms, 24
  Broccoli with Tofu and Shiitake Mushrooms, 31
  Mushrooms with Pasta, Red Wine, and Thyme, 67
  Mushrooms with Shiitake Cream Sauce, 65
  varieties listed, 64
  Zucchini Stuffed with Shiitake Mushrooms, 104

N

Nuts, 54
  Candied Walnuts, 50

O

Onions, 11
  Onion Caramelized Tart, 69
  Onions Stewed with a Biscuit Crust, 70
Orange Sauce for Wok-Seared Broccoli, 32
Orange Wok Sauce, 13
Oyster Sauce Wok Sauce, 13

P

Parsnips, 84
  with Orange, Cinnamon, and Chile (substitute), 102
  Parsnips in Gingered Orange Sauce, 71
Pasta
  Grilled Eggplant Lasagna, 49
  Mushrooms with Pasta, Red Wine, and Thyme, 67
  Smoked Tomatoes Tossed with Fusilli Pasta, 96

Peas
   Pea Soup with Garlic and Cheese Croutons, 73
   Stir-Fried Snow Peas with Ginger-Butter Glaze, 87
Peppers, 11. *See also* Chiles
   Artichoke and Roasted Red Pepper Tart, 20
   Peppers with Caribbean Curry and Grand Marnier, 76
   Pizza with Roasted Pepper Topping, 74
Pickles
   Cucumbers Pickled with Garlic and Chiles, 46
Pizza with Roasted Pepper Topping, 74
Poaching, 15
Potatoes, 11
   Mashed Potatoes with Garlic and Horseradish Root, 79
   with Orange, Cinnamon, and Chile (substitute), 102
   Potato Gratin with Roasted Garlic, 77
Pot-Stickers, Spinach, 88
Pressure-cooking, 18
Pumpkin, 92
   Pumpkin Soup with Cilantro Swirl, 80

R
Radicchio Salad with Bananas and Avocados, 82
Ratatouille, Thai Eggplant, 47
Risotto, Carrot, 36
Roasting, 10–11
Root vegetables, 84–85. *See also specific vegetables*
Rutabagas, 85

S
Salad dressings
   Blue Cheese Dressing, 55
   Creamy Lemon Garlic Dressing, 55
   Ginger Herb Dressing, 55
Salads, 54–55
   Asparagus Salad with Pine Nuts, 23
   Endive Salad with Candied Walnuts and
      Papaya Nests, 50
   Fennel Salad with Mango-Walnut Herb
      Dressing, 52
   Green Bean Salad with Ginger-Soy Dressing, 56
   Jicama Tex-Mex Salad, 60
   Radicchio Salad with Bananas and Avocados, 82
   Roasted Beet Salad with Fresh Mozzarella
      Cheese, 29
   Sprout Salad with Hot Wok Dressing, 91
   Tomatoes in All Their Glory, 98
   Watercress with Orange Segments and Warm
      Goat Cheese, 101
Salsas
   Chile Mango Salsa, 40
   Tomato Salsas, 99
Sauces. *See also* Salsas
   Asian-Cajun Dipping Sauce, 22
   Asian Hollandaise Sauce, Brussels Sprouts with, 34
   for batter-fried vegetables, 17

Coconut Wok Sauce, 13
   Orange Sauce, for Wok-Seared Broccoli, 32
   Orange Wok Sauce, 13
   Oyster Sauce Wok Sauce, 13
   Spicy Asian Butter Sauce, 22
Sautéing, 14
Shiitake mushrooms. *See* Mushrooms
Short-cooking vs. long-cooking vegetables, 12
Snow Peas, Stir-Fried, with Ginger-Butter Glaze, 87
Soups
   Celery Root Soup with Ginger and Herbs, 39
   Pea Soup with Garlic and Cheese Croutons, 73
   Pumpkin Soup with Cilantro Swirl, 80
   Thai Corn Soup with Chile-Jam Accent, 43
Soybeans, 26, 27
Spinach
   Spinach Pot-Stickers, 88
   Wok-Seared Spinach, 90
Sprout Salad with Hot Wok Dressing, 91
Squash, 92. *See also* Summer squash; Winter squash;
   Zucchini
Steaming, poaching, and blanching, 15
Stir-fry dishes
   Broccoli with Tofu and Shiitake Mushrooms, 31
   Stir-Fried Bok Choy with Mushrooms and
      Peppers, 30
   Stir-Fried Cauliflower with Mediterranean
      Accents, 38
   Stir-Fried Snow Peas with Ginger-Butter Glaze, 87
   Stir-Fried Szechwan Green Beans, 57
   Wok-Seared Broccoli with Orange Sauce and
      Pine Nuts, 32
   Wok-Seared Spinach, 90
Stir-frying, 12–13
Stock, Vegetable, 19, 107
Summer squash, 11, 92. *See also* Zucchini
   Grilled Summer Squash, 95
   Sautéed Summer Squash in Asian-Creole Cream
      Essence, 94
   Stir-Fried, with Mushrooms and
      Peppers (substitute), 30
Sweet potatoes, 11, 85

T
Tarts
   Artichoke and Roasted Red Pepper Tart, 20
   Onion Caramelized Tart, 69
Techniques for cooking vegetables, 10–18
Tempura, 16–17
   All-Purpose Tempura Batter, 17
   Tempura Batter with Egg and Baking Soda, 17
Thai Corn Soup with Chile-Jam Accent, 43
Thai Eggplant Ratatouille, 47
Thai-Inspired Tomato Salsa, 99
Tomatoes, 11

Smoked Tomatoes Tossed with Fusilli Pasta, 96
   Tomatoes in All Their Glory, 98
   Tomato Salsas, 99
Turnips, 85
   with Orange, Cinnamon, and Chile (substitute), 102

V
Vegetable Stock, 19, 107

W
Walnuts, Candied, Endive Salad with Papaya
   Nests and, 50
Watercress with Orange Segments and Warm Goat
   Cheese, 101
Winter squash, 11, 92
   Acorn Squash Stuffed with Dried Fruit and Grand
      Marnier, 93
   Pumpkin Soup with Cilantro Swirl, 80
Wok cooking, 12–13. *See also* Stir-fry dishes

Y
Yams, 11
   Yams with Orange, Cinnamon, and Chile, 102

Z
Zucchini. *See also* Summer squash
   with Tofu and Shiitake Mushrooms (substitute), 31
   Zucchini Blossoms Stuffed with Goat Cheese, 103
   Zucchini Stuffed with Shiitake Mushrooms, 104

More Hot Cookbooks by Hugh Carpenter & Teri Sandison

Fifty bold and sophisticated yet easy stir-fry recipes seasoned with a host of exciting ingredients. Perfect ideas for fresh, healthy weeknight meals or weekend entertaining. Includes more than fifty vibrant color photos.

Fifty wild and zesty recipes that combine chicken with the distinct flavors and cuisines of the world. Discover delicious and elegant ways to serve one of the most versatile and healthy meats. More than fifty color photos provide dramatic presentation ideas.

Fifty fresh and sensational recipes that take pasta to new and dazzling heights. Packed with easy, inventive ideas, this is the complete resource for busy cooks at all levels of experience. Includes more than fifty exciting color photos.

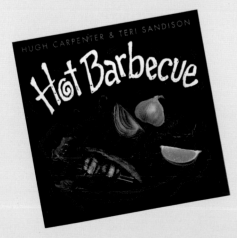

Fifty sizzling recipes for classic barbecue favorites and innovative pleasers from around the world. From simple any-night delights to elaborate weekend feasts, this latest tantalizing offering in the ever-popular Hot series will heat up backyards and kitchens alike.